ALPHA STORIES

Learning the alphabet through flannelboard stories

by
Mary Beth Spann

Art by
Debby Dixler

FIRST TEACHER PRESS
First Teacher, Inc./ Bridgeport, CT

ACKNOWLEDGEMENTS

I wish to extend my deepest respect and gratitude to the following master teachers and storytellers: Claire Blatchford, Viki Diamond, Dr. Lazar Goldberg, and Michael O'Donoghue. By sharing their gifts and insights, they opened my mind and heart to the magic of storytelling. Without them, this book would not have been written.

ISBN 0-9615005-6-5

Library of Congress Catalog Card Number 87-083159

Design by Karen Baumann

Cover Design by Alice Cooke; Cover photo by Hester Holbrook Abrams

Editor: Lisa Lyons Durkin

Assistant Editor: Kathleen Hyson

Typesetting and layout: Michael Pearl, Michael Durkin

Manufactured in the United States of America

Published by First Teacher Press
First Teacher, Inc. P.O. Box 29, 60 Main Street, Bridgeport, CT 06602

Distributed by: Gryphon House, Inc.
                P.O. Box 275
                Mt. Ranier, MD 20712

Table of Contents

WE BELIEVE THAT

- Storytelling is a powerful teaching tool guaranteed to touch children's minds and hearts.

- The flannelboard can help enrich and extend the storytelling experience.

- Storytelling with the flannelboard involves children in the storytelling process by offering them a visual prop that can last beyond the actual story telling experience itself.

- Storytelling with the flannelboard helps develop story sequence and comprehension skills. Follow-up discussions and activities encourage creative thinking skills.

- The flannelboard and story pieces together comprise an ideal quiet learning center for directed or independent play. Here, readiness skills for reading and math may be introduced in a setting that is as comfortable as a bedtime story.

Introducing
Alpha Stories

Alpha Stories is a unique collection of original stories and flannelboard patterns designed to help familiarize young children with alphabet letters and sounds. Our specially created flannelboard pieces help bring letters and sounds to life, while providing you and your children with story manipulatives for follow-up fun. In addition, *Alpha Stories* provides you with hints and suggestions for making story-telling a true learning experience.

Included with each story are comprehension and discussion questions that help little minds to think big. Also included are story-related projects and activities which reinforce a variety of important concepts and help build a solid readiness foundation for subsequent learning.

Above all else, *Alpha Stories* is an invitation for you and your children to share the warmth and wonder of story-telling. Together, you will be creating magical memories that will last happily ever after.

- Read each story to yourself before presenting it to your children. For a true storytelling experience, you should attempt to retell the story in your own words; however, you may instead wish to read the story to your group.
- The stories may be shared with or without the flannelboard pieces. You may want to make flannelboard pieces for only a select number of stories—perhaps those stories representing vowel sounds or stories that prove popular with your group. ("The Green Ghost" is the only story which must be presented on the flannelboard for the storyline to make sense.)
- Your flannelboard should be large enough to accommodate all of your pieces without crowding. When a commercially made flannelboard is not available, one can easily be constructed from a large length of black felt or flannel stretched and stapled securely to a piece of plywood cut to a desired size. (See page 12.)
- Before beginning, pile your story pieces together in order of appearance. As each flannelboard object and character is introduced, place it on the flannelboard. Continue to point and refer to it as often as the story does.
- After each story, use the discussion questions to evaluate how well your children understood the story line and concepts. The questions are open-ended to encourage individual responses and reactions. Remember that listening to a story is a very personal experience.
- To better involve the children, retell the story while allowing them to hold and place the pieces when appropriate. This promotes good listening skills and increased attention spans.
- After sharing a story twice, challenge your children to tell you the story all by themselves (You can give hints, if necessary.)
- For freetime fun, allow children to stick favorite story pieces on the flannelboard. Children should be encouraged to imitate your storytelling efforts and retell their own versions of the story for each other.

HOW TO MAKE A FLANNEL BOARD

1. FROM THIN PLYWOOD, THICK CARDBOARD, OR TRI-WALL (AVAILABLE AT ART SUPPLY STORES), CUT A 2' X 3' RECTANGLE.

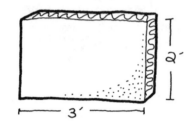

2'

3'

2. MEASURE A PIECE OF FLANNEL OR LIGHTWEIGHT FELT (BLACK IS TRADITIONAL, BUT OTHER COLORS WORK WELL, TOO) TO FIT. THE DIMENSIONS OF THE BOARD PLUS 6 EXTRA INCHES ON ALL 4 SIDES (2'6" X 3'6"). SNIP CORNERS OF FABRIC.

SNIP

SNIP

BOARD

FELT OR LIGHTWEIGHT FLANNEL

SNIP

SNIP

3. PLACE FLANNEL OR LIGHTWEIGHT FELT ON FLOOR, RIGHT SIDE DOWN. STRETCH BORDER TO BACK OF BOARD, CREATING A SMOOTH COVERED SURFACE. TACK FABRIC TO BACK OF BOARD WITH INDUSTRIAL STRENGTH STAPLES OR THUMB TACKS.

4. IF DESIRED, SECURELY TACK A SMALL NYLON ROPE HANDLE TO TOP OF COMPLETED FLANNEL BOARD FOR STORAGE PURPOSES AND PORTABILITY.

Making and Storing the Flannelboard Pieces

The flannelboard patterns included in this book have been designed with a variety of construction possibilities in mind. The main flannelboard pieces for each story appear as full-sized patterns. Optional pieces appear as smaller-sized patterns which can easily be enlarged during construction. Color suggestions appear next to many pattern pieces, but feel free to experiment with color choices of your own.

On a copy machine, duplicate the flannelboard patterns in this book and use as cutting guides. First, lay the duplicated paper shape on felt. Next, using a fineline felt-tipped marker, trace around the shape. (When using smaller patterns, trace a wide margin around the shape to enlarge the size of the felt piece you want to create.) Finally, use a sharp scissors to cut out the felt shape.

Some story pieces are pictured with optional patterns for clothes and accessories which may be cut from felt or fabric and glued directly on top of the felt pieces. Solid-colored felt pieces may also be decorated with marker, yarn, or fabric scraps. (Guard against making your felt pieces too heavy or they will not adhere to the flannelboard.) Details may also be added to felt flannelboard pieces with colored fineline felt-tipped markers. Correction fluid may be effectively used to highlight many features (eyes, claws, toenails, and so on). Eyes may also be cut directly from the duplicated pattern page and glued onto the felt piece giving characters an appealing animated look.

EDWARD THE ENORMOUS ELEPHANT—
USE CORRECTION FLUID TO MAKE TOENAILS.

To construct paper flannelboard pieces directly from the pattern pages, use a copy machine to duplicate patterns, then use crayons or markers to outline and color in the drawings. Back these paper pieces with felt, flocked adhesive paper (often available in hardware stores), or bits of sandpaper, and cut out. (For durability, you may wish to cover paper pieces with a clear adhesive paper before backing and cutting.)

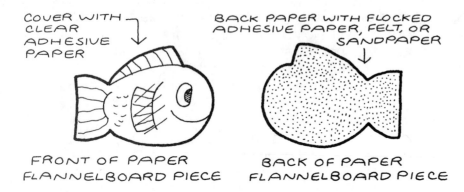

COVER WITH CLEAR ADHESIVE PAPER

BACK PAPER WITH FLOCKED ADHESIVE PAPER, FELT, OR SANDPAPER

FRONT OF PAPER FLANNELBOARD PIECE

BACK OF PAPER FLANNELBOARD PIECE

For storage and protection, place each set of story pieces into individual file folders or zip-locking plastic bags. Label each bag with story title and page number. These bags may be tacked to a bulletin board or hung from a ceiling wire, thus allowing for easy access. To avoid a mixup of story pieces, allow children to play with only one story at a time.

For a more permanent storage system, place the plastic bags inside file folders or manilla envelopes. Store these flat or in a file cabinet to avoid having the pieces mash together and become wrinkled or torn.

For extra fun and reinforcement, copy a set of story patterns for each child to color and cut out. These, along with a copy of the story itself, can then be placed in an envelope and sent home with instructions for a family story sharing.

CARLA THE CRAFTY CAT
PAGE

FLANNEL STORY STORAGE

The Flannelboard as a Learning Center

Unlike a book, the flannelboard cannot be easily turned for viewing pleasure. Before beginning, make certain that everyone has a comfortable, unobstructed view. (This can help everyone to be a good listener, too.)

• Patterns of people and animals may be copied, colored, cut out and glued to craft sticks to serve as the basis for a stick puppet collection.

• Using the suggestions for making paper pieces, children can make flannelboard cutouts of their friends, family members, or community helpers. Place these on the flannelboard and have children describe or create dialogue for the characters.

• Using popular children's book illustrations as a guide, create flannelboard pieces that depict familiar characters that you have read about together. Allow children to retell the story using the story pieces. (Offer cues where necessary.)

• If you're working on a unit involving geometric shapes (or if you're in a hurry and need story pieces in a jiffy), substitute the simple shapes for complex cutouts. For example, three white squares of decreasing size could represent the Three Billy Goats Gruff or a red rectangle could pose as Little Red Riding Hood.

• While telling a story, experiment with a "stop action" method of inquiry. Right before reaching the climax portion of the story, pause and challenge the children to predict what will happen next. Be sure to always satisfy your listeners with the "real" ending to the story. Compare and contrast your conclusions , making certain to praise any and all prediction efforts.

• With adult supervision, offer capable children a supply of felt and adult scissors. Encourage them to create their own felt shapes for the flannelboard. Younger children may enjoy decorating pre-cut felt shapes with markers, sequins, and felt bits.

• Song lyrics become more understandable to young children when spelled out rebus-style with flannelboard characters. Encourage reluctant vocalists to participate by choosing them to assemble the song pieces on the board as they harmonize.

- Fingerplays and rhymes become a hands-on experience when displayed on the flannelboard. After the poem is recited, ask your children if they can pick rhyming pairs or opposites off the board.

- Grab discarded children's books from your school or public library, cut out the illustrations and use as flannelboard pieces. If you have two copies of the same book, one can be used for reading and the other (older copy) may be cut apart and displayed.

- Magazine pictures, photographs, and cartoons can all serve double duty when prepared as flannelboard pieces. Comic strips (which can be cut apart and rearranged on the board) are great for developing sequence skills. Large magazine pictures can be cut apart, reassembled puzzle-style, and displayed on the board for someone else to try.

- For a lesson on the concept of "part-to-whole", cut apart pictures (or felt silhouettes) of body parts, animals, plants, and vehicles. Prepare pieces for the flannelboard. Have children match parts together to create whole pictures.

- Using geometric shapes or story pieces with an observable theme, create a pattern for children to complete. Verbalize exactly what you expect them to find, "*Here is a red circle and a green circle, and a red circle and a green circle. Find what comes next in this pattern.*" (If using story pieces, try beginning a simple pattern like this, "*Here is a bird and a piece of bread, and a bird and an apple, and a bird and a carrot. What comes next?*")

• Using any flannelboard pieces that are handy, play a process of elimination game. Begin by placing all of the pieces on the board. Then, tell your children that you are thinking of *one* piece, and offer clues and guesses until the incorrect pieces are eliminated and the mystery piece is found. (*"I am thinking of an animal with four legs. "* (Remove any people and bird pieces.) *"I. am thinking of a furry animal."* "(Remove the pig and the turtle pieces.) *"I am thinking of an animal that barks. Yes! My piece is the dog."*)

• Use your flannelboard as a weather station. Each day, post child-created symbols signifying the day's weather. You may also decide to "dress" a flannel weather boy or girl in appropriate clothes for the elements. As you leave for the day, predict the followings day's weather on the flannelboard, and keep a bar graph noting correct and incorrect predictions.

• To strengthen visual memory and recall, place any number of flannelboard pieces on the board. Tell children that you are going to remove a piece and that they will have to guess which piece is missing. Obviously, the more pieces on the board, the more difficult it will be to guess which piece has been hidden. To avoid participant frustration and to insure each child a measure of success, the level of difficulty may differ for each one.

• Back the photographs from a field trip with felt and display on the flannelboard for all to enjoy. Challenge your class to reorganize the pictures in the order that they were taken.

• On paper, draw simple pictures of cooking ingredients and tools from your latest recipe. After enjoying the recipe, review the steps for preparation with the flannelboard pieces.

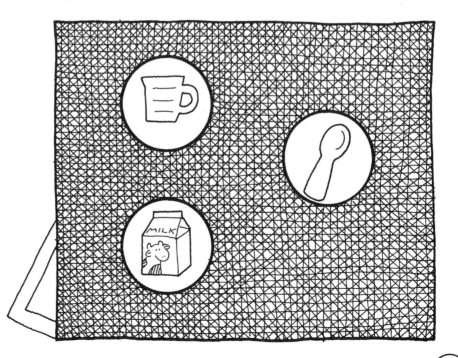

Freeplay Fun
with the Flannelboard

The flannelboard is a wonderful freeplay center that should be made available to children throughout the year.

If you have very limited space and cannot display the flannelboard at all times, show your children where they can go to retrieve it from storage if they want to use it. Remember, the flannelboard can be opened on the floor and propped against a wall with pieces stored in a box beside it—it doesn't need fancy accommodations.

An organized storage system should protect your pieces, but they will get wear and tear from children's unsupervised use. It's wise for you to demonstrate to your children exactly how you want the pieces to be handled and stored. Impress upon them that you will be willing to share your things only if they will be cared for properly.

Allow children to play with only one story or set of pieces at a time. This rule will help keep your story sets from becoming hopelessly mixed up.

In the event that your filing and storage system does need some updating, enlist some of your more responsible children to help with the searching and sorting process. (A list of pieces taped to the inside of each bag will make this chore much easier.)

To avoid traffic jams at the flannelboard, allow only two children to use it at one time. Children are marvelously inventive when it comes to the flannelboard—when given story pieces to play with, they can quietly amuse themselves for long periods of time without interruption and without teacher direction. Stifle your urge to "show the child how to play." If you want to join in the child's freeplay fun, allow him to take the role of the teacher and you may be his eager-to-please student.

Don't be surprised if the undirected child imitates many of the adult-directed activities you've shared with your group. This is just the child's way of digesting, experiencing, and controlling what has been a pleasurable learning experience.

The Ant and the Apple

Once upon a time, there lived a little ant named Anthony who didn't know what to give his teacher Ms. Atom for her birthday. Anthony thought and thought, and finally, he had a good idea. *"I'll bring her an apple,"* he said. *"Teachers always love apples!"*

So, early one morning before school, Anthony walked all the way to the apple orchard, and sure enough, there on the ground was a nice, juicy, red apple that had just fallen from the tree. It would be perfect for Ms. Atom!

Just then, some bigger ants on their way to school saw Anthony and asked him what he was doing.

"I want to bring an apple to my teacher," said Anthony. *"I'm just trying to figure out how to move this apple all the way to school."*

"Ha, ha, ha!" laughed the bigger ants. *"You can't move that apple to school. You can't, you can't!"*

Anthony's feelings were hurt, but he took a deep breath and said, *"Never say 'can't' to an ant!"*

First, Anthony tried pushing on the apple with his right legs. The apple didn't move.

"You can't; you can't!" laughed the bigger ants.

"Never say 'can't' to an ant!" shouted Anthony.

Next, Anthony tried pulling on the apple with his left legs. The apple didn't move.

"You can't, you can't!" laughed the bigger ants.

"Never say *can't* to an ant!" shouted Anthony.

Finally, Anthony tried pushing and pulling on the apple with all six of his legs. The apple still didn't move.

"You can't; you can't!" laughed the bigger ants. And then, they left for school. For one second, Anthony worried that maybe the bigger ants were right. But then Anthony had another good idea. He began breaking off little pieces of the apple and carrying them to school, one by one. When he was done, he put the pieces in a jar with honey and cinnamon and mashed everything together. He closed the jar lid tight and decorated it with a birthday ribbon.

School was just about to begin when a tired Anthony arrived at his class. The other ants had piled their presents on Ms. Atom's desk. There were apricots and airplanes and even an alphabet book. But the sweetest, most amazing gift of all was a jar of Anthony Ant's applesauce. On the jar was a birthday ribbon, and tied to the ribbon was a little message that said:

"Never say *'can't'* to an ant!"

ALPHABET BOOK

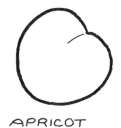

APRICOT

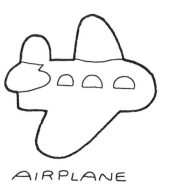

AIRPLANE

Comprehension Questions

• What did Anthony Ant want to bring to his teacher? Why was it difficult for him to move the apple?
• Why did the bigger ants laugh at Anthony? How did Anthony feel when they laughed at him? Why?
• How did Anthony try to move the apple? How did Anthony finally solve his problem?
• Has someone ever make fun of you or hurt your feelings? How did you feel? What did you do?

Follow-up Activities

Study Ants

On a warm day, go outside and watch ants at work. Sprinkle crumbs for the ants to carry. Consider making homemade ant farms. Consult a children's librarian for books with directions for making ant farms.

Make Applesauce

Have children break apples into tiny pieces with clean fingers. Place pieces into blender with honey and cinnamon to taste. Blend and enjoy!

Make Cardboard Ants

Cut corrugated cardboard into ant shapes. Point out head, thorax, and abdomen to children. Have them paint the ants red, brown, or black; when dry, push pipecleaner legs through holes in cardboard, bend, and stand. An extra pipecleaner may serve as antennae.

APPLE

ANTHONY ANT-DARK GREY FELT

PANTS FOR
ANTHONY ANT-
BRIGHT FELT
OR FABRIC

DRESS FOR
MS. ATOM-
BRIGHT FELT
OR FABRIC

MS. ATOM-
DARK GREY FELT

A

Never
say
CAN'T
to an
ant!

BIRTHDAY RIBBON AND TAG-
FOR APPLESAUCE JAR

APPLESAUCE JAR-YELLOW FELT

EYE PATTERN
FOR ANTS-CUT
1 PER ANT
(TOTAL 5)-
WHITE PAPER

GROUP OF
BIGGER ANTS-
DARK GREY FELT

Ben Bunny and the Bluebird

Once upon a time, there lived a little brown bunny named Ben. Now, since Ben Bunny was always hungry, he was always looking for food. Many times, if he looked hard enough, he could find his favorite foods like ripe berries on a bush, bib lettuce behind the barn, or even breadcrumbs in the backyard.

But this time, tired Ben Bunny was having no luck. He looked and looked for something to nibble on, but it was the middle of winter and everything was frozen and still. Ben was just about to take his empty bunny tummy back into his bunny hole, when suddenly, he heard a strange noise. He picked up his long rabbit ears to give a better listen. YES--there it was again! Someone was crying for help! Ben forgot all about being tired and hungry. He began to search around for a clue, and it wasn't long before he found the noisemaker--on a frozen bench lay a poor bluebird whose wing was bruised.

From the soft bark of a nearby tree, Ben made a bandage for the hurt wing.

"You'll soon be good as new," said Ben Bunny as he turned to hop away.

"Wait!" chirped the grateful bluebird in his tiny voice. *"You have been so kind to help me--let me help you in return. I am a magical bird. For your kindness, I can grant you one wish."*

Ben looked at the bird more closely. Ben saw a magical twinkle in the bird's eye and he knew that the bird was telling the truth.

Ben was very excited about having his wish come true, but he thought very carefully so that he would make the best choice possible. He began to think of bunches of berries and barrels of bib lettuce. He even thought about bananas and buns and beans (even jelly beans). It was difficult to decide what to wish for; but, first he wanted to thank the bluebird for the wish.

"Thank you for giving me this wonderful wish," said Ben Bunny, reaching one paw out to pat the bird's sore wing. *"I only wish you were all healed so that you could fly home with me now."*

As soon as these words were spoken, the bluebird's wing was totally healed and he could fly again. Then, Ben Bunny realized that he had used his one and only wish to get his new friend well.

While Ben was very happy to see that his wish had made his friend well, he still felt sorry for himself and his poor, empty tummy.

"Please don't be sad, Ben Bunny," begged the bluebird. *"Your kindness has healed my hurt wing, and now I can fly all over the land and gather the tastiest food you ever tasted. As long as I am able to fly, you will never go hungry again."*

And the two friends--the bird and the bunny--spent many happy years being kind and helpful to each other and everyone they met.

BUN

BEANS

JELLY BEANS

Comprehension Questions

• What was Ben Bunny looking for in the beginning of the story? Why did he stop looking?

• Why was Ben able to hear the tiny bluebird's cry for help? What did Ben do to help the bird?

• When Ben was granted his magic wish, what did he *really* want to wish for. Did Ben *want* to use his wish to help the bird get better? How do you know?

• If you were given one wish, what would you wish for?

Follow-up Activities

Do the "Bunny Hop"

Your local library can help you dig up an old recording of "The Bunny Hop" dance to share with your class. Before dancing, you might want to make bunny ears and cotton tails to jazz up your act.

Discuss Animal Eating Habits

Talk about why Ben Bunny was having such a hard time finding food in the winter, and discover how some animals cope with scarce food supplies during the rough winter months-- hibernation, migration. Are there ways that people can help animals--birds, squirrels--live through such weather more comfortably?

Create "Wish Books"

After asking your children to share their most important wishes with the group, have the children illustrate their wishes on star-shaped paper. Staple the wishing stars together into booklets and have children decorate the booklet covers with gold and silver glitter. For future reading (and wishing) reference, you may want to print the dictated wishes beneath each illustration.

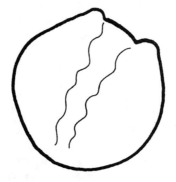

BIB LETTUCE-
LIGHT GREEN FELT

BEN BUNNY - BROWN FELT
OPTIONAL: GLUE ON COTTON BALL FOR TAIL AND STRING PIECES FOR WHISKERS.

EYE PATTERN FOR BEN BUNNY - WHITE PAPER; CUT 1.

BLUEBIRD - WITH "TWINKLE" IN HIS EYE.

BEAK FOR BLUEBIRD - YELLOW FELT

EYE PATTERN FOR BLUEBIRD - WHITE PAPER; CUT 1.

"CLAWS" FOR BLUEBIRD - YELLOW FELT

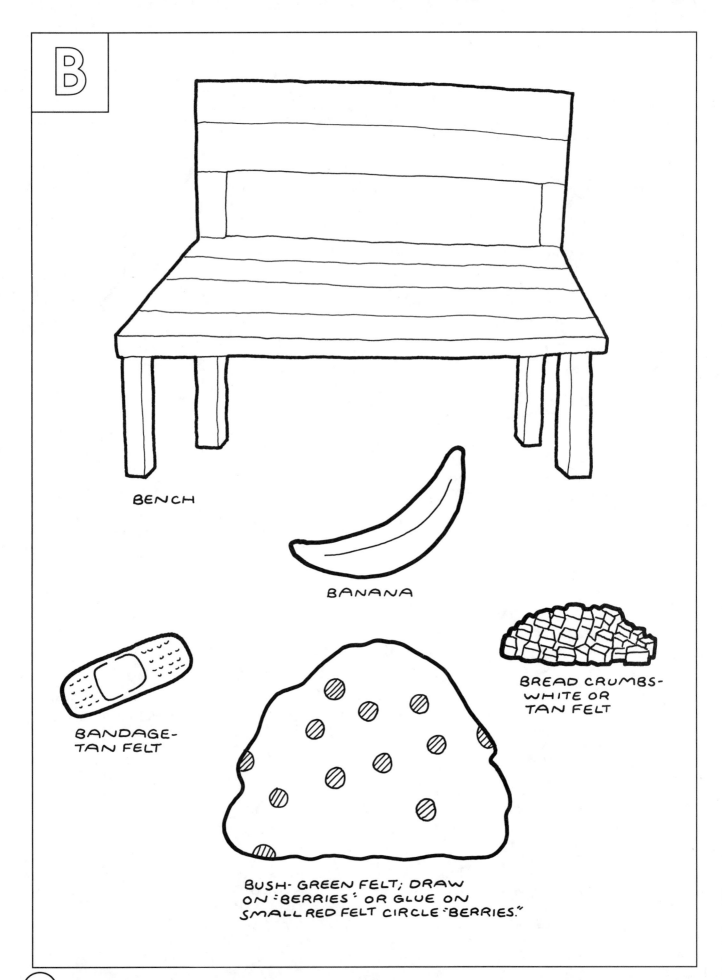

B

BENCH

BANANA

BANDAGE-
TAN FELT

BREAD CRUMBS-
WHITE OR
TAN FELT

BUSH- GREEN FELT; DRAW
ON "BERRIES" OR GLUE ON
SMALL RED FELT CIRCLE "BERRIES."

Carla the Crafty Cat

Once upon a time, there was a crafty cat named Carla. Carla wanted to have a party for all of her friends, but she did not want to do any of the work for the party.

"I know what I'll do," thought Carla, *"I'll trick my friends into doing part of the work . Then, I can curl up and relax."*

First, Carla Cat called her friend Carol Caterpillar. *"I'm having a party at Cat Cottage,"* said Carla, *"and I want you to come. I do have one teenie-tiny favor to ask you. Would you please clean my Cat Cottage for the party?"* she purred.

"Yes, I will come to your party at Cat Cottage," said Carol Caterpillar, *"but I am too busy trying to find a spot to spin my cocoon to help you clean Cat Cottage."*

"If you clean my cottage," said Carla Cat, *"I will look for a spot for you to spin your cocoon."* And so it was settled.

Next, Carla Cat called her friend Craig Canary. *"I'm having a party at Cat Cottage,"* said Carla, *"and I want you to come. I have one teenie-tiny favor to ask you. Would you please bake a carrot cake for the party?"* she purred in her cutest cat voice.

"Yes , I will come to your party at Cat Cottage," said Craig Canary, *"but I am too busy cleaning my canary cage to bake a carrot cake for your party."*

"If you will bake a carrot cake for the party," said Carla Cat, *"I will clean your canary cage."* And so it was settled.

Last, Carla called her friend Cathy Cow. *"I'm having a party at Cat Cottage,"* said Carla, *"and I want you to come. I have one teenie-tiny favor to ask you. Would you please drive your car to the store on the corner to get cans of cranberry juice for my friends to drink?"* she purred in her cutest cat voice.

"Yes, I will come to your party at Cat Cottage" said Cathy Cow, *"but I am too busy caring for my baby calf to drive my car to the store on the corner to get cans of cranberry juice."*

"If you will drive your car to get cans of cranberry juice , " said Carla Cat, *"I will care for your baby calf,"* And so it was settled.

Everyone kept their promises. On the morning of the party, Carol Caterpillar cleaned Cat Cottage, Craig Canary baked a carrot cake, and Cathy Cow drove her car to the store on the corner to get cans of cranberry juice for the friends to drink.

Meanwhile, Carla Cat left her cottage in search of a spot where Carol Caterpillar could spin a cocoon; then, she went to Craig Canary's house to clean his canary cage; and finally she went to Cathy Cow's barn to care for Cathy's baby calf. When she was done, Carla Cat went back to Cat Cottage. She was very tired, so she checked her clock and noticed that she had just enough time for a catnap before the party was to begin.

Later that day, when Carla Cat's friends arrived with the carrot cake and the cans of cranberry juice for the party, they found Carla curled up on the couch, and no matter how hard they tried, they couldn't wake her up. So, they cleaned the cottage, and had the party without her.

CANS OF CRANBERRY JUICE

CARROT CAKE

CLOCK

29

Comprehension Questions

• What did Carla Cat *not like* to do? Do you like to do work at your house? What jobs do you do at home? What jobs do you wish you could do?
• In the story, which friend did Carla Cat call first? What job did Carla ask that friend to do? What job did Carla Cat promise to do for that friend?
• Who did Carla Cat call next? What job did Carla ask that friend to do? What job did Carla Cat promise to do for that friend?
• Who did Carla Cat call last? What job did Carla ask that friend to do? What job did Carla Cat promise to do for that friend?
• If you had been invited to Carla's Cat's party, would you have helped her to do her work? Which job in the story would be the most fun? The least fun?
• Why was Carla Cat so tired in the end of the story? What could she have done so that she would have been awake for her party? Was Carla as crafty as she thought she was?

Follow-up Activities

Create a Cat Cottage

Make a pattern of Cat Cottage and provide each of your children with two identical paper cottage pieces which have been stapled together at one side. With scissors or craft knife, adult cuts four windows in top sheet of house. Child then "opens" windows and draws story characters onto house shape beneath. When faces are completed, child opens the entire front of the house and completes drawing the inside of Cat Cottage. Remind children to draw as many letter C pictures in the house as they can think of--couch, cake, closet, cans, carpet, carrots, cobwebs, cookies, coats, candle, cactus.

Clean Up and Celebrate

Discuss the importance of having everyone share in a workload. Discuss various jobs that everyone has at home and in school. Make a chart listing both jobs that are *fun* to do--using spray cleaner on the table--as well as jobs that are *yucky* to do--cleaning up your room. End this dialogue with a clean-up committee designed to give everyone a chance to pitch in and help. After your classroom, tables, shelves or playspaces are all spic and span, congratulate your cooperative efforts with a carrot cake and cranberry juice celebration!

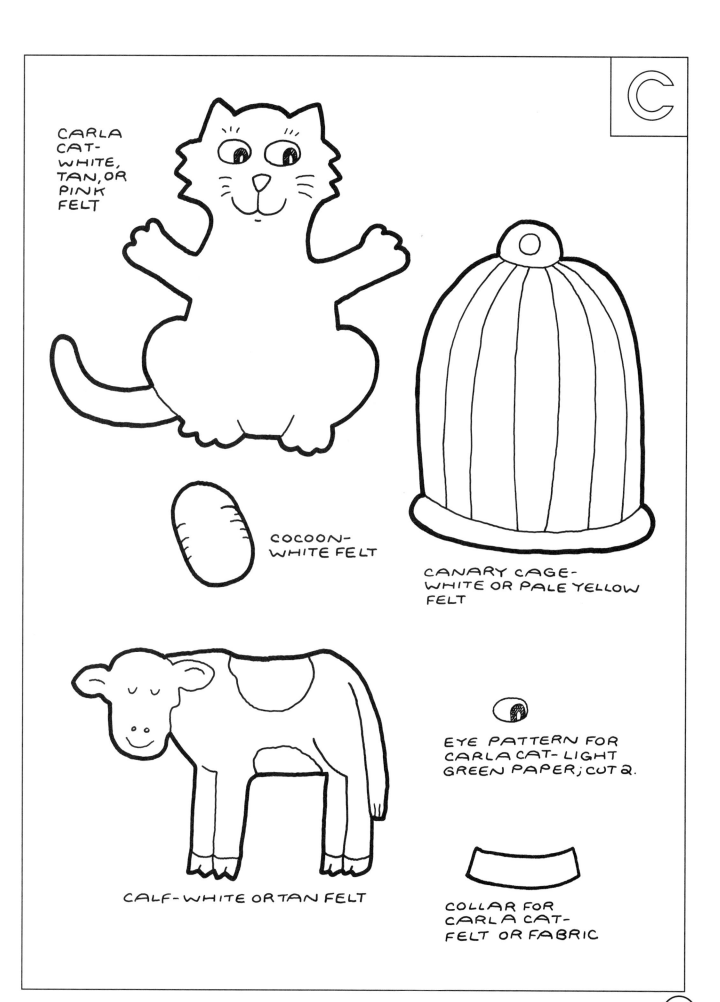

CARLA CAT- WHITE, TAN, OR PINK FELT

COCOON- WHITE FELT

CANARY CAGE- WHITE OR PALE YELLOW FELT

EYE PATTERN FOR CARLA CAT- LIGHT GREEN PAPER; CUT 2.

CALF-WHITE OR TAN FELT

COLLAR FOR CARLA CAT- FELT OR FABRIC

EYE PATTERN FOR
CAROL CATERPILLAR,
CRAIG CANARY, AND
CATHY COW-WHITE
PAPER; CUT 1 FOR
EACH (3 TOTAL).

CRAIG
CANARY—
YELLOW FELT

CAROL CATERPILLAR-GREEN FELT

CATHY
COW-
WHITE
OR TAN
FELT

Debbie Dragon's Difficult Dinner (D)

Once upon a time, there was a little dragon named Debbie. Debbie Dragon did not like to eat dinner.

"Now, Debbie," said Mother Dragon, *"how do you expect to grow up big and strong if you do not eat your dinner?"*

Debbie did not want to eat the dragon stew that Mother Dragon had made for dinner.

""M-M-M-M...Smell that good dragon stew," said Mother Dragon. *"Smell the dandelions and the daisies? Smell the doggie biscuits and the dill pickles? You don't know what you're missing!"* Mother Dragon declared. *"Be a good little girl dragon and try some for me."* And with that, Mother Dragon took a big dipper of dragon stew and poured it into Debbie Dragon's deep dish.

"Disgusting!!" exclaimed Debbie Dragon and she stuck out her fiery tongue.

"Now, Debbie," frowned Mother Dragon, *"if we don't like something, we just say 'No, thank you'."*

"No, thank you," said Debbie, and she pushed her dish away. *"Mommy, I want doughnuts,"* she added.

"Doughnuts are dessert for good little dragons who finish all of their dragon stew," said Mother Dragon. *"Dragon stew first, doughnuts later."*

But Debbie did not want to eat her dragon stew; so, when Mother Dragon was not looking, Debbie Dragon did a very naughty thing. When Mother Dragon was not looking, Debbie Dragon fed her dragon stew to her dragon dog. And then, she told a lie.

"Mommy, I ate all of my dragon stew," fibbed Debbie. *"May I please have my doughnut now?"*

"Yes, Debbie," smiled Mother Dragon. *"You may have one doughnut now that you've finished your dragon stew."*

So, Debbie ate one doughnut. But, Debbie was still hungry, so she ate *one dozen* doughnuts. That's *twelve* doughnuts in all!

By bedtime, Debbie told Mother that her tummy hurt. *"I don't think it was dragon stew that make you sick,"* said Mother. *"It was probably that one little doughnut you ate that hurt your tummy."* Mother Dragon used a dropper to give Debbie some drippy medicine that really *did* taste disgusting, and Debbie Dragon fell asleep knowing that she would never again try to trick her Mommy. And she would never, ever again want to eat another doughnut.

Comprehension Questions

• Why did Debbie Dragon think that dragon stew for dinner was disgusting? Are there any foods that you don't like to eat? What do you do when your Mommy or Daddy asks you to try those foods?

• Was Mother Dragon being mean when she wanted Debbie Dragon to eat her dragon stew? What would you do if your child would not eat the foods that are good for growing?

• Why did Debbie feed her dinner to her dog? Would you do this with your dinner?

• In the end of the story, Debbie Dragon decides to never trick her mother again. Why does she decide this? Why does Debbie also decide never, ever again to eat another doughnut? Do you think she'll change her mind? Why?

Follow-up Activities

Plan a Dragon Dinner

Using paper plates, have children cut out pictures of "D" words and paste onto the plates. Orally, share your dragon delicacies. (Remind the children that dragons are pretend fire-breathing creatures, so what they eat is up to their imagination.) This same activity can be used to plan delicious dinners for people and may include attention to the four food groups that are recommended for good growing.

Discuss Dishonesty

In the story, Debbie Dragon is dishonest. What does "dishonest" mean? What does "honest" mean? Why was Debbie Dragon dishonest? Is it ever O.K. to tell a lie? Is it a good idea to be honest? Why?

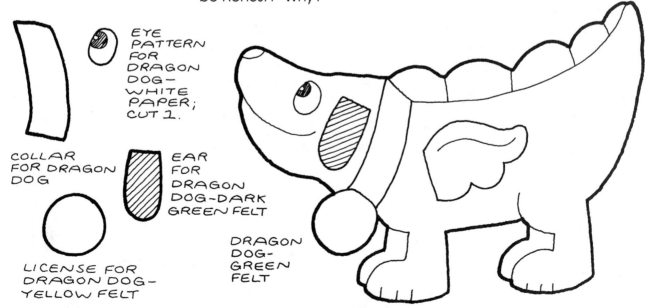

EYE PATTERN FOR DRAGON DOG – WHITE PAPER; CUT 1.

COLLAR FOR DRAGON DOG

EAR FOR DRAGON DOG–DARK GREEN FELT

LICENSE FOR DRAGON DOG– YELLOW FELT

DRAGON DOG– GREEN FELT

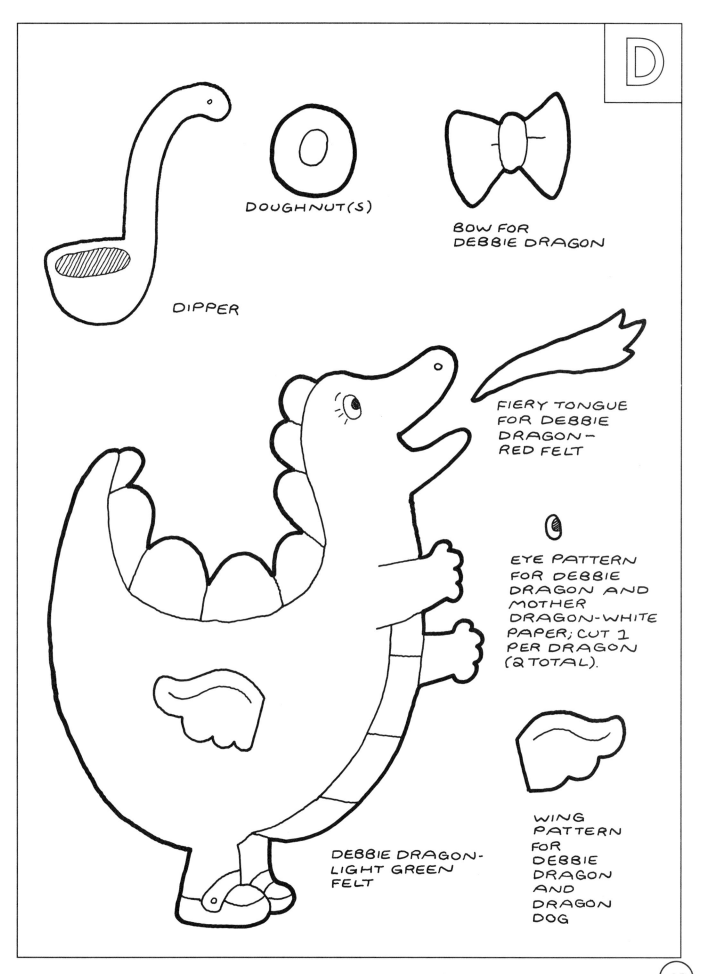

DOUGHNUT(S)

BOW FOR
DEBBIE DRAGON

DIPPER

FIERY TONGUE
FOR DEBBIE
DRAGON -
RED FELT

EYE PATTERN
FOR DEBBIE
DRAGON AND
MOTHER
DRAGON-WHITE
PAPER; CUT 1
PER DRAGON
(2 TOTAL).

DEBBIE DRAGON-
LIGHT GREEN
FELT

WING
PATTERN
FOR
DEBBIE
DRAGON
AND
DRAGON
DOG

D

D

NECKLACE
FOR
MOTHER
DRAGON

WING PATTERN
FOR MOTHER
DRAGON

MOTHER
DRAGON-
LIGHT
GREEN
FELT

DEEP
DISH

DROPPER

36

The Enormous Elephant

Once upon a time, there was an enormous elephant named Edward. Edward grew and grew because he loved to eat eclairs and Eskimo pies. And, he loved to drink eggnog.

Of course, Edward did have some problems because of his size. Each morning, Edward had no energy. (It took a lot of extra energy for enormous Edward to get up and move around.) Each evening, Edward was exhausted. All that extra fat made him feel very tired. But Edward Elephant just kept on growing until the day came when Edward found out that he could no longer fit even one enormous ear into the elevator that took him up to his apartment on the eleventh floor. This meant that Edward would have to climb up eleven flights of stairs to get to his apartment--and Edward *hated* to climb stairs!

Edward decided to talk to his good friend Elton the Elf. Elton Elf also lived on the eleventh floor of the apartment building, but he was not enormous or exhausted like Edward. Instead, Elton was small and energetic. He ate foods like egg salad, English muffins, enchiladas, and egg rolls. He even ate eggplant.

"The first thing you have to do," said Elton, *"is to give up eclairs and eggnog. You have to eat energy food that will help your body feel good. Then, you have to do more exercise to lose weight and feel energetic."*

Edward Elephant did not want to stop eating eclairs and eggnog. He did not want to exercise. But he knew that Elton Elf was just trying to help, so he said to himself, *"I'll listen to Elton Elf for just one week, and then I'll tell him that his idea isn't working."*

So, Edward Elephant listened to Elton Elf for just one week. On Sunday, he ate egg salad instead of eggnog. On Monday, he ate eggrolls instead of eclairs. On Tuesday, he ate English muffins instead of Eskimo pies. On Wednesday, he ate eggplant instead of marshmallow eggs. And, on Thursday, Friday, and Saturday, he went with Elton Elf to exercise in the park. At the end of the week, he was hungrier and more exhausted than ever! He told Elton Elf, *"I quit!"*

"Before you quit," replied Elton, *"see if you can fit into the elevator a bit easier than before."*

Edward tried fitting into the elevator. He *could* fit one enormous ear into the elevator, and he became excited!

"Maybe I shouldn't quit just yet," decided Edward.

And so, for eleven weeks after that, Edward Elephant and Elton Elf ate and exercised together. Edward Elephant began to feel less enormous and more energetic. Every week, Edward could fit more and more of himself into the elevator until finally every extra inch of elephant fit in with room to spare.

But Edward Elephant no longer wanted to ride up in the elevator to the eleventh floor. He was feeling too energetic for that. Besides, he wanted some exercise, so he raced Elton Elf to the eleventh floor. Can you guess who won?

Comprehension Questions

• Why was Edward Elephant so enormous? Why was he always so tired and exhausted? What made him want to change his size?

• What kind of elf was Elton? Was he a good friend to Edward? How do you know?

• Was it easy for Edward to stop eating so much food? How do you know? Have you ever done something that was very hard for you to do? How did you feel?

• In the end of the story, Edward is at last able to fit in the elevator. Why does he decide to race up the stairs? Who won the race? How do you know?

Follow-up Activities

Compile a List of Enormous Things

On a large chart, list all of the enormous things you and your children can think of. Begin with elephants, and move on to monstrosities such as skyscrapers, dinosaurs, and jumbo jets. (The sky's the limit here!) After you've collected your huge assortment, try and rank them from smallest to largest.   If an argument regarding relative size erupts, you may need to consult with an encyclopedia for a final authority.

Cook Up an Energy Food Feast

Whip up a batch of egg salad with the group, spoon it onto beds of endive lettuce, and serve with English muffins. While they're munching away, tell the group about the benefits of each food and why each is important for energy.

Exercise

Visit your local library, and borrow some exercise records produced especially for children. After exercising with the children, discuss with them how their bodies felt before and after the exercise sessions. Point out that different exercises help the body in different ways (Streching exercises are helpful in keeping muscles limber, while aerobic exercise helps tone the heart and lungs.)

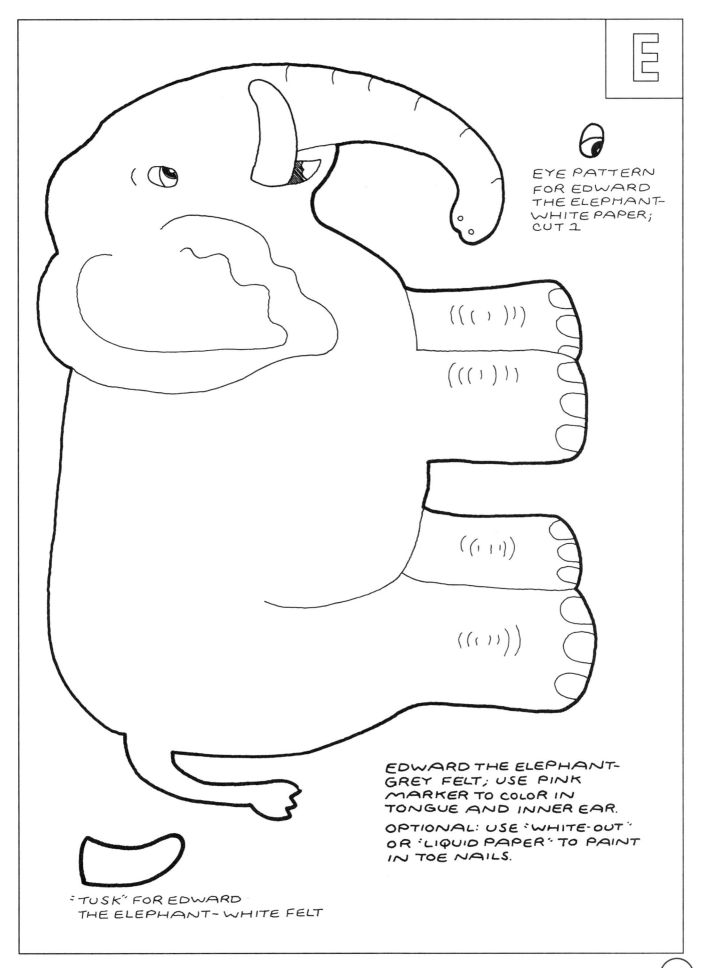

E

EYE PATTERN
FOR EDWARD
THE ELEPHANT—
WHITE PAPER;
CUT 1

EDWARD THE ELEPHANT—
GREY FELT; USE PINK
MARKER TO COLOR IN
TONGUE AND INNER EAR.

OPTIONAL: USE "WHITE-OUT"
OR "LIQUID PAPER" TO PAINT
IN TOE NAILS.

"TUSK" FOR EDWARD
THE ELEPHANT—WHITE FELT

EYE PATTERN
FOR ELTON
ELF-WHITE
PAPER; CUT 2.

ELTON ELF-
LIGHT
GREEN
FELT

BOW TIE
FOR
ELTON
ELF-
FELT OR
FABRIC

ENGLISH
MUFFIN-
WHITE
FELT

ECLAIR-PALE
YELLOW FELT;
USE BROWN MARKER
TO DRAW ICING.

EGG NOG-
YELLOW
FELT

EGG PLANT-
PURPLE FELT

EGG SALAD
(IN SANDWICH)-
WHITE FELT; USE YELLOW
MARKER TO COLOR
EGG SALAD FILLING.

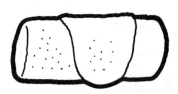

EGG ROLL-
TAN FELT

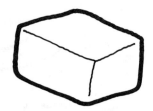

ESKIMO PIE-
BROWN FELT

Freddy the Forgetful Fish

Once upon a time, there was a little fish named Freddy. One day Father Fish said to Freddy, *"It's time now that you went to school."*

Father Fish told him the way to go: *"Remember, Freddy, to get to the fish school, you have to swim below the frogs and behind the ferns. And, whatever you do, keep far, far away from flies on fish hooks ."*

Freddy promised to remember Father Fish's words, and he set off swimming toward fish school. For a little while, Freddy remembered Father Fish's directions, and as he swam along, he said them over and over again:

"Swim below the frogs and behind the ferns and keep far, far away from flies on fish hooks." Then, Freddy began to forget what Father Fish had told him. Instead, he began to say: *"Swim above the frogs and in front of the ferns and keep far, far away from flies on fish hooks."*

Just when Freddy was getting very tired of trying to find fish school, he saw something shiny dangling in the water above his head. It was a fish hook and, on the hook was a nice, juicy fly. *"I think Father Fish said to swim toward the fish hook,"* thought Freddy, so that's just what he did. In one gulp, he swallowed the fly and fish hook. He was quickly pulled up onto the shore by two friends who were fishing there.

"Hey! Look we caught a fish!" said the boy named Frank.

"It's a beauty!" said the girl named Fay.

They took the hook out of Freddy's mouth and set him on the ground nearby.

"Hello!" said Freddy. *"How are you?"* Freddy thought he was in school, so he tried his best to be friendly.

Frank and Fay were surprised to hear Freddy talk, but they were friendly, too, and spent the rest of the day visiting with Freddy. When it was time for Frank and Fay to go home, they had become good friends with Freddy the Fish, and they decided to set him free.

Freddy couldn't wait to swim home and tell Father Fish about all of the fun he had that day. *"Father Fish will be so proud of me for remembering how to get to fish school,"* thought Freddy. *"I hope I remember how to get there again tomorrow!"*

FROG-
LIGHT
GREEN
FELT

41

Comprehension Questions

• Why did Father Fish want Freddy Fish to go to fish school?
• Where did Father Fish tell Freddy Fish to swim to help him get to fish school? Why did Freddy Fish get lost?
• Did Freddy Fish get to school? How do you know?
• What do you think Father fish will say when he hears how Freddy spent his day?

Follow-up Activities

Make a "School of Fish" Display

Enlarge the flannelboard fish shape to a desired size, then offer each child a pre-cut (or pre-traced) shape to decorate. Provide the children with a variety of decorative scraps (Yarn, foil, cellophane, rick-rack, and buttons work well.), then show the children how fish scales, eyes, and gills may be drawn or placed on the paper fish. When finished, display the fish on a bulletin board which has been prepared with a blue-and-white paper backdrop cut to represent waves and sky.

Play "Gone Fishing"

Introduce children to the sound of the letter "F," then have them search through magazines for pictures of objects that begin with that sound. With (or without) adult assistance, have the children cut out the pictures, and paste them onto pre-cut paper fish shapes. Place a paperclip onto the mouth of each fish, and place fish into an imaginary pond in the middle of the floor. By dangling the magnetic "hook" of their fishing pole (made by tying a small magnet to a string and then attaching the string to a dowel or yardstick) over the pond, children take turns catching and identifying " F fish." Older children may want to use the name of the picture in a sentence.

Get Hooked on Fish

Your children's library can help you catch the latest on fishy facts and fantasy. After enjoying popular fish tales (Fish are widely featured characters in children's literature.), children will enjoy pouring over pictures of exquisite fish varieties, and may enjoy a trip to a local tropical fish store. Remember, also, that a freshwater fish makes a perfect classroom pet.

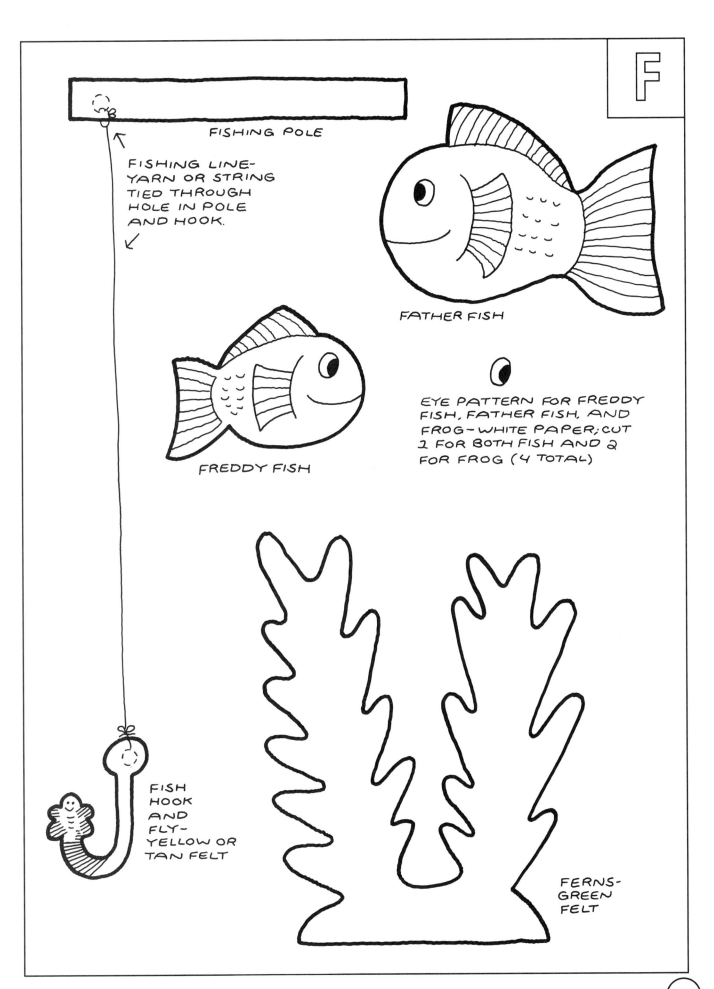

FISHING POLE

FISHING LINE-
YARN OR STRING
TIED THROUGH
HOLE IN POLE
AND HOOK.

FATHER FISH

FREDDY FISH

EYE PATTERN FOR FREDDY
FISH, FATHER FISH, AND
FROG-WHITE PAPER; CUT
1 FOR BOTH FISH AND 2
FOR FROG (4 TOTAL)

FISH
HOOK
AND
FLY-
YELLOW OR
TAN FELT

FERNS-
GREEN
FELT

F

F

EYE PATTERN FOR
FRANK AND
FAY-WHITE
PAPER; CUT 2
FOR BOTH (4
TOTAL)

PANTS FOR FRANK AND
FAY-FELT OR FABRIC

FRANK

FAY

SWEATSHIRTS FOR FRANK
AND FAY-FELT OR FABRIC

The Green Ghost

Once upon a time, there lived four ghosts in a haunted house. Now, three of these ghosts were the regular kind: spooky and white. The fourth ghost was different: he was not spooky and he was not white. He was green!

The white ghosts teased and laughed at the green ghost. They sang a song to hurt his feelings (sung to the tune of "Mary Had a Little Lamb"): *"You are not a scary ghost, scary ghost, scary ghost. You are not a scary ghost, so we'll all laugh at you-- BOO!"*

Finally, the green ghost could stand the teasing no longer. He went to visit his friend, Gregory Gray Squirrel. He sang him this song: (sadly, and to the same tune): *"I am not a scary ghost, scary ghost, scary ghost. I am not a scary ghost. I can only say BOO HOO!"*

"You would be scarier if you were white," agreed Gregory. *"I don't know how to help you, but let me take you to Great Gorilla. He may have an idea!"*

The green ghost followed Gregory Gray Squirrel deep into the woods. Pretty soon, they reached the home of Great Gorilla. When Gregory explained the problem to Great Gorilla, the gorilla's eyes glowed. *"Follow me!"* he shouted, and the green ghost had to fly very fast to catch up.

When the three friends finally stopped, they were in front of an old, broken-down garage.

"Whoever lives here will just make fun of me, too." whispered the green ghost sadly.

"This is a special house," said Great Gorilla, *"and here comes the ghost who lives here."* A smiling white ghost landed among the friends.

"Would you like to help me haunt this house?" he asked the green ghost.

"I'm green, not white," the green ghost replied. *"Who will be afraid of me?"*

"Follow me and see," said the white ghost. So the green ghost followed the white ghost inside the house and when they both peeked out of the windows, they both looked the same to Gregory Gray Squirrel and Great Gorilla outside-- very green and very scary. The windows of the house were made of green glass.

That Halloween, the little green ghost had such fun howling at the witches and the cats that went by. He even sang a new song as he danced happily in his new home (To the tune of "Jingle Bells"): *"I am green, I am green, I am green, not white. But, I can be happy now because I am a fright. OH! Halloween, Halloween, how I love you so. Halloween is so much fun to scare those folks we know."*

Comprehension Questions

• Why was the little green ghost so unhappy? What did the other ghosts do to make him feel sad?

• Who did the little green ghost visit when he could no longer stand being teased? Why do you think the green ghost picked a friend to share his problem with?

• Who did Gregory Gray Squirrel take the little green ghost to see? Was Great Gorilla able to help the little green ghost?

• Where did the little green ghost go in the end of the story? Why was this a good place for the green ghost to be? Do you think the green ghost will ever go back to see the three white ghosts?

Follow-up Activities

Fingerpaint Green Ghosts

Using sheets of fingerpaint paper, draw one large ghost on the back of each sheet. On the glossy side of the paper, place one tablespoon of blue paint, and one tablespoon of yellow paint. Direct children to mix the paints with their hands to get a new color (green). When paintings are dry, cut out ghost shapes using guidelines on back. Decorate with wiggle eyes and use wallpaper scraps for hats and jewelry.

Gobble Goodies

Make a ghost salad with green lettuce and green grapes sprinkled with granola. Serve with grape juice and graham crackers.

Grate Green Crayons

Place a length of waxed paper on a folded towel or ironing board. Show children how to grate green (and other colored) crayons onto paper. Cover with an identical size sheet of waxed paper and a towel folded for double thickness. On low setting, iron on the towel, causing crayons to melt and fuse paper together. Trim finished papers neatly, punch hole in top, and thread with ribbon for a window hanging.

GREGORY
GRAY
SQUIRREL

PATTERN FOR GREAT GORILLA FACE - PINK OR TAN FELT

GREAT GORILLA - BROWN FELT

GREEN GHOST - BRIGHT GREEN FELT

EYE PATTERN FOR GREEN GHOST AND GREGORY GRAY SQUIRREL - WHITE PAPER; CUT 1 FOR BOTH (2 TOTAL).

MEAN, WHITE GHOSTS - CUT 3 : DRAW EYES DIRECTLY ON FELT

KIND, SMILING WHITE GHOST - DRAW EYES DIRECTLY ON FELT.

HAUNTED HOUSE

① CUT SHAPE OUT OF TAN FELT.

② CUT ALONG BROKEN LINES TO OPEN WINDOWS AND DOOR.

③ TAPE PIECES OF GREEN CELLOPHANE BEHIND WINDOW OPENINGS SO WINDOW "PANES" APPEAR GREEN.

Once upon a time, the parts of the body had a meeting to decide who was most important.

The head spoke first: *"I protect the brain which does all of the important thinking. I have many other special body parts--eyes for seeing rainbows, ears for hearing a bird's song, a nose for smelling supper cooking,and a mouth for tasting warm, delicious meals. Without me, life would be sad, indeed. Clearly, I'm the most important part of the body!"*

The heels spoke second: *"You forget about us heels because we're always at the bottom of things, but we help the body stand up, push pedals on a bicycle or dance a jig. Without us, life would be sad, indeed. Clearly, heels are the most important part of the body!"*

The hands spoke third: *"Hands are special, too! We help people draw pictures for Grandma, tie laces on sneakers, or hug each other tight. Without us, life would be sad, indeed. Clearly, hands are the most important part of the body!"*

The hips spoke forth: *"We're important because we hold the legs to the body. We help people twist around when someone calls them from behind, and we help the legs kick a ball down the street. Without us, life would be sad, indeed. Clearly, hips are the most important part of the body!"*

The heart spoke last: *"My job is to pump rich, red blood to every part of the body. I travel to the head, the hands, the hips, and the heels. I know that you all need me and my blood, but I need all of you, too. I need heels to help me exercise, hips to help me sit down and rest, the head to make decisions for me, and hands to help hold someone else's heart close so that I'm not lonely. I think that we're all important in our own way!"*

And all of the body parts agreed and got back to work.

Comprehension Questions

• Why did the body parts have a meeting? What parts were at the meeting?
• Why did the head think she was most important? Heels? Hands? Hips? Heart?
• Why did the heart say that she needed another heart close sometimes? Who do you hug when you don't want to be alone?
• Which body parts do you think are most important?

Follow-up Activities

Play "Simon Says"

Challenge children to touch these body parts--eyebrows, shins, palms, calves, crowns, knuckles, shoulder blades, spine. Remind the class to only move when the direction is prefaced by the command "Simon Says!"

Develop Body Awareness

With children, jog in place for twenty seconds and have them observe the change in heart rate. Have children take a deep breath and observe expanded lung capacity. Have them swivel on hips and notice rotation ability. Together, make a list of "Things Hands Can Do."

Make "Hands On" Display

Place length of brown butcher paper over bulletin board or wall. In colorful letters, paint the words "Hands-On Art," and have children fill paper with multi-colored handprints. Have children dip their whole hand in one color, fingers in contrasting colors. Help them wipe excess paint off hand before printing.

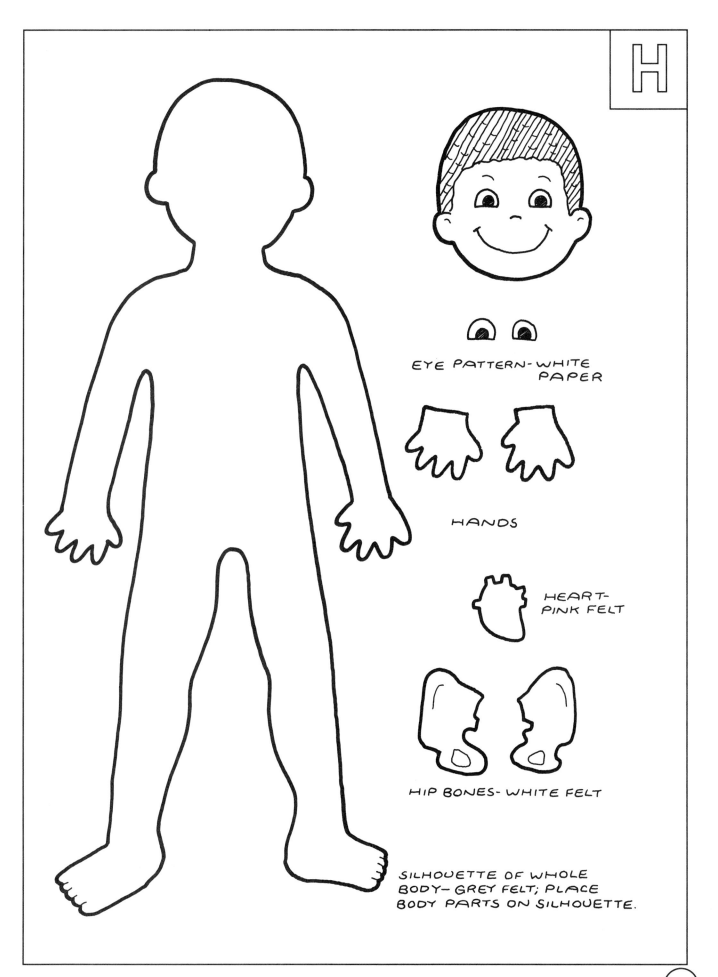

EYE PATTERN-WHITE PAPER

HANDS

HEART-PINK FELT

HIP BONES- WHITE FELT

SILHOUETTE OF WHOLE BODY— GREY FELT; PLACE BODY PARTS ON SILHOUETTE.

H

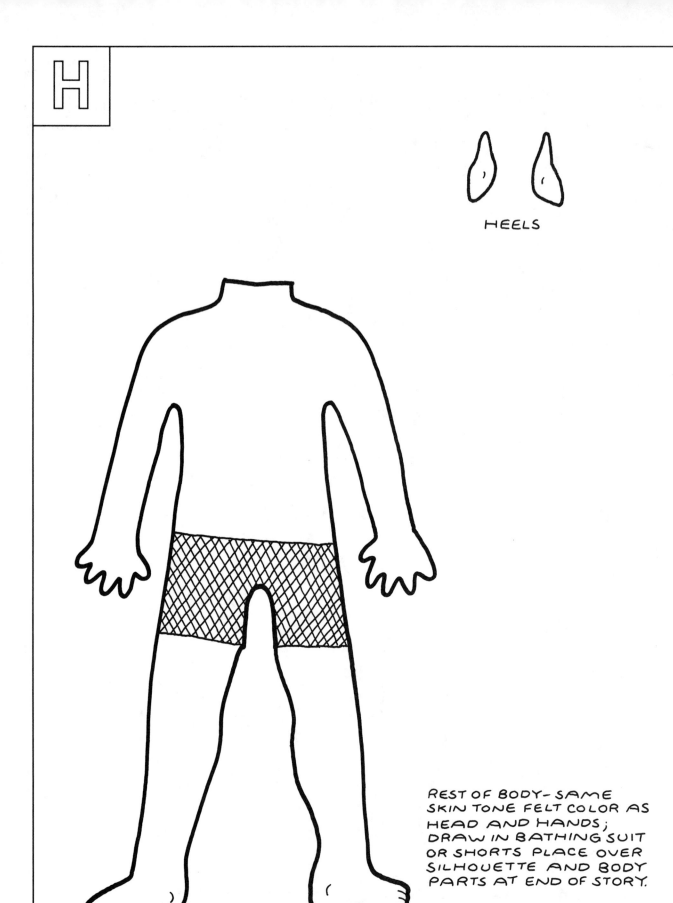

HEELS

REST OF BODY— SAME
SKIN TONE FELT COLOR AS
HEAD AND HANDS;
DRAW IN BATHING SUIT
OR SHORTS PLACE OVER
SILHOUETTE AND BODY
PARTS AT END OF STORY.

Inchy the Inchworm

Once upon a time, there was an inchworm named Inchy. Inchy was little and cute, but she was also mean. She called the other inchworms nasty names like *"icky"* and *"idiot."* They didn't want to play with her at all.

Deep down, Inchy was very sad. She wanted to make friends, but she didn't know how. Inchy was afraid to let the other inchworms know she was sad, so instead, she acted nasty.

Inchy's father, Ichabod Inchworm, was very worried about his little girl. He decided to help Inchy make some new friends, so he sent this invitation to all of the other inchworms:

> *Dear Friends,*
> *Please come to my house on Saturday.*
> *We will play games and have snacks.*
> *Yours Truly,*
> *Inchy Inchworm*

The other inchworms were happy to read their invitations. They thought that Inchy was finally able to be friendly. They told Inchy that they wanted to come to her house on Saturday.

Inchy wasn't sure why the other inchworms were being so friendly. But she was so happy that company was coming that she just smiled.

On Saturday, the inchworms came to visit Inchy. They played games and sang songs. They ate Mr. Inchworm's igloo-shaped cake with icing. Inchy was not icky or mean--instead she was all smiles.

Finally, it was time for everyone to leave. They all promised to come again next Saturday.

When Inchy and her father were alone again, they had a talk. *"I don't know why the inchworms decided to visit me Daddy,"* said Inchy. *"But, at least, they were finally able to be friendly!"*

Comprehension Questions

• What was Inchy Inchworm's problem? Why was she so mean to the other inchworms? How did they feel about Inchy?
• What kind of a father was Mr. Inchworm? How did he try to help Inchy?
• What did the inchworms think when they got their invitations? Who really sent the invitations?
• How did Inchy feel when she found out the other inchworms were coming to her house? How did she behave at the party? How will Inchy behave next Saturday when the inchworms visit again?

Follow-up Activities

Measure in Inches

Show your children the length of an inch on a ruler, then provide them with pieces of paper one square inch in size. Have children measure common objects in the room by laying the squares end to end and counting the number of papers needed to cover or correspond in length to the object. (Do not aim for exact measurement skills here; measurement concept is more important.)

Make Inchworm Prints

Help children dip yarn in green paint--styrofoam trays work well--and lay on brown paper. Allow to sit for five seconds; then, have them lift yarn straight up, being careful not to smear paint. Have children do this many times to simulate inchworms on tree bark.

Learn More About Inchworms

Share pictures of real inchworms with your group. Discuss what life might be like as an inchworm; then, make a list entitled "Interesting Inchworm Facts." Display this list surrounded by your inchworm prints.

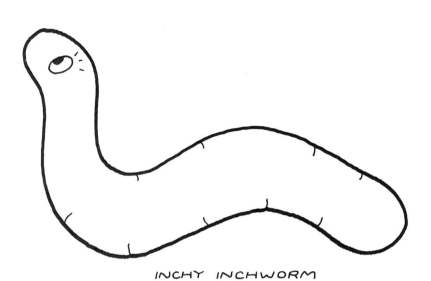

INCHY INCHWORM

EYE PATTERN
FOR INCHY
INCHWORM-
WHITE PAPER

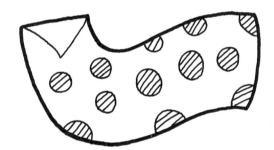

DRESS FOR INCHY INCHWORM-
BRIGHT FELT OR FABRIC

CHERRY
FOR TOP
OF IGLOO
CAKE
(OPTIONAL)

IGLOO CAKE-
WHITE FELT

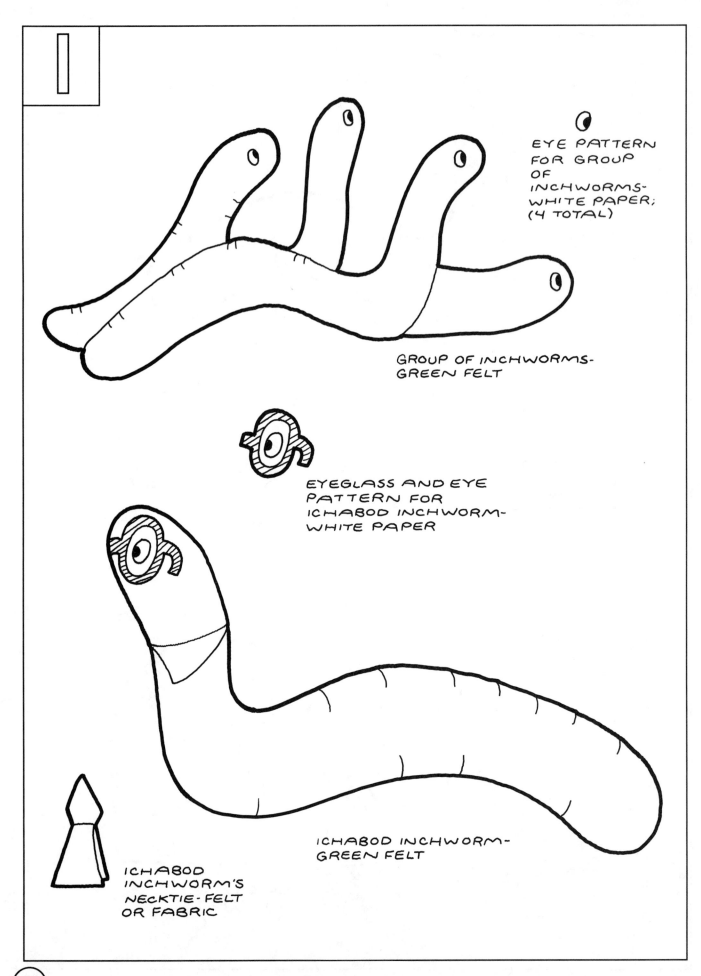

EYE PATTERN
FOR GROUP
OF
INCHWORMS-
WHITE PAPER;
(4 TOTAL)

GROUP OF INCHWORMS-
GREEN FELT

EYEGLASS AND EYE
PATTERN FOR
ICHABOD INCHWORM-
WHITE PAPER

ICHABOD INCHWORM-
GREEN FELT

ICHABOD
INCHWORM'S
NECKTIE-FELT
OR FABRIC

Julie and the Jellybeans

Once upon a time, there was a jellyfish named Julie who loved jellybeans. Julie's mother, Mrs. Jellyfish, kept a jar of juicy, jumbo jellybeans on the shelf in the kitchen. In the jar was a red jellybean, a green jellybean, a yellow jellybean, a pink jellybean, a blue jellybean, an orange jellybean, and a black jellybean. Julie was not allowed to eat any jellybeans unless her mother said it was O.K.

One day in June, Julie asked her mother if she could have a jellybean. *"Next Sunday is the first day of July. It is your birthday and, on that day you may eat one jellybean,"* said Mrs. Jellyfish.

Julie was very excited. Today was Sunday, so she would have to wait seven more days until her birthday next Sunday. *"How will I be able to wait that long until my birthday?"* thought Julie. *"And how will I know which jellybean tastes best?"*

Julie thought and thought. She stared at the seven jellybeans in the jar. Then, before she knew it, Julie grabbed the jar, opened it up, and popped a red jellybean into her mouth. *"I'll only eat this one,"* she promised herself, but then...

On Monday, she ate a green jellybean.
On Tuesday, she ate a yellow jellybean.
On Wednesday, she ate a pink jellybean.
On Thursday, she ate a blue jellybean.
On Friday, she ate an orange jellybean.
On Saturday, she ate a black jellybean.

And by Sunday, Julie's birthday, July 1st, there were no jellybeans left in the jar.

On the morning of her birthday, Julie's mother came to wake her up. *"Happy birthday, Julie,"* she sang. *"Today's the day you may have your jellybean. You may bring me the jar."*

But, when Julie brought Mother the jellybean jar, it was empty. "I'm sorry, Mother," said Julie. *"I ate one jellybean each day this week. There are none left for my birthday."*

"Julie," said Mother, *"I'm sorry you ate all the jellybeans--now you have no treat for your birthday. Maybe next year on your birthday, you will be able to have a jellybean--because that's how long you'll have to wait for me to fill the jar again!"*

JELLY BEANS-

CUT 1 IN
FOLLOWING
COLORS:
PINK, BLUE,
YELLOW,
GREEN,
BLACK,
ORANGE

J

Comprehension Questions

• What food did Julie Jellyfish love? Where did Mrs. Jellyfish keep the jellybeans? When was Julie allowed to eat jellybeans?
• When was Julie's birthday? How many days did she have to wait until her birthday? Is it hard to wait for a birthday to come? Why?
• Why did Julie eat the jellybeans? Why did she only eat one each day? If you were Julie, would you have eaten the jellybeans? Why or why not?
• In the end, Mother Jellyfish tells Julie that she will not fill her jellybean jar for a whole year! Is this fair?

Follow-up Activities

Play Jellybean Math

Using jar and jellybean pieces from the story, place a number of jellybeans in the jar for your group to count. Add more and have them count the new total. Take some away and have them count the new total. Every time an amount is added or subtracted, the numerical amount should be stated aloud. ("*I am adding three more jellybeans. How many do we have all together?*")

Have a Jellybean Race

Place a jellybean on a spoon and have each child carry his spoon to a predetermined destination without dropping the jellybean. The child may eat a jellybean when the task is completed, and may have an endless number of tries. (Give the children fresh jellybeans to eat, rather than those being carried and dropped.)

Paint Jellyfish

Enlarge jellyfish flannelboard pattern onto oaktag and place in a shallow box. Fill empty egg carton containers with small amounts of paint and have children drop jellybeans in paint, turning until coated. Remove paint-coated jellybeans from carton, place in box on jellyfish shape. Have children turn and tilt box until jellybeans make interesting patterns on the fish. Dry and display. (A marble may be used instead of a jellybean.)

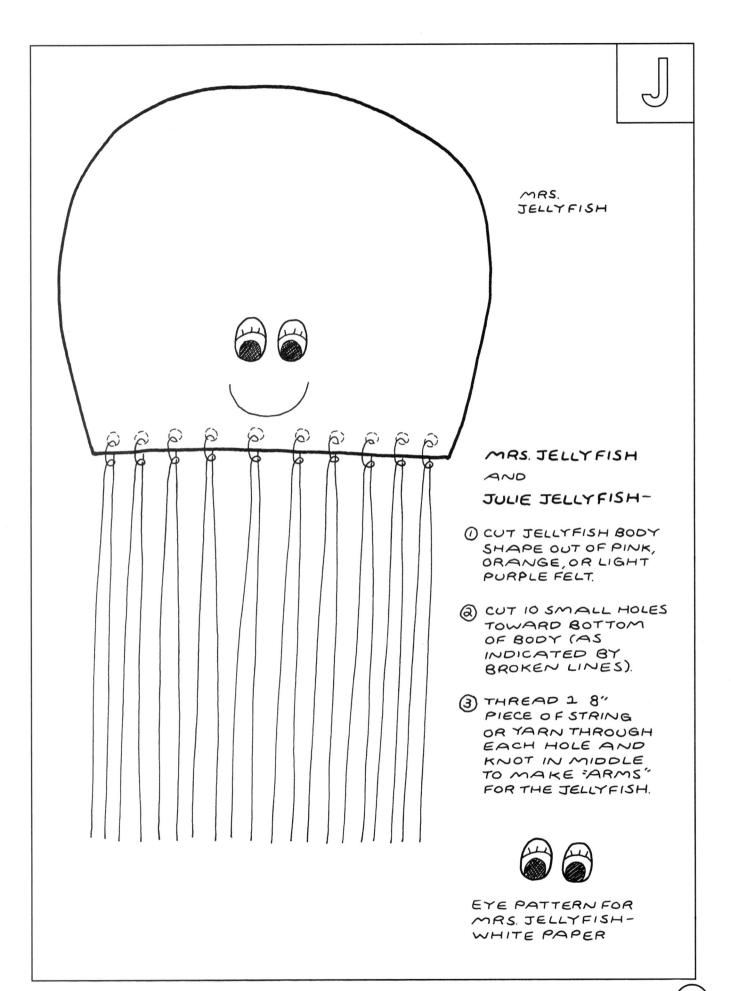

MRS.
JELLYFISH

MRS. JELLYFISH
AND
JULIE JELLYFISH—

① CUT JELLYFISH BODY
SHAPE OUT OF PINK,
ORANGE, OR LIGHT
PURPLE FELT.

② CUT 10 SMALL HOLES
TOWARD BOTTOM
OF BODY (AS
INDICATED BY
BROKEN LINES).

③ THREAD 1 8"
PIECE OF STRING
OR YARN THROUGH
EACH HOLE AND
KNOT IN MIDDLE
TO MAKE "ARMS"
FOR THE JELLYFISH.

EYE PATTERN FOR
MRS. JELLYFISH—
WHITE PAPER

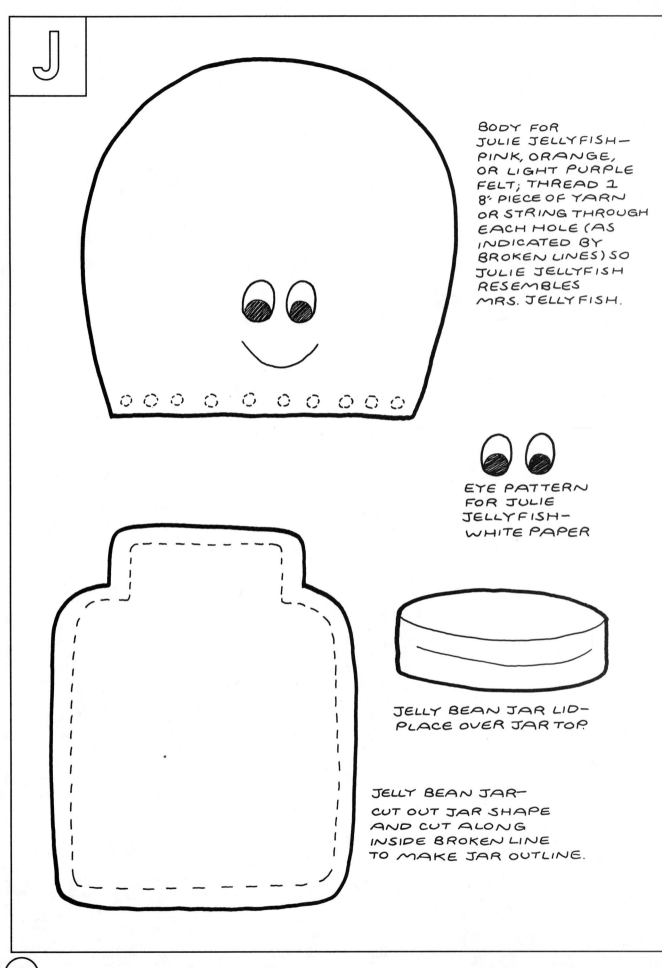

BODY FOR
JULIE JELLYFISH—
PINK, ORANGE,
OR LIGHT PURPLE
FELT; THREAD 1
8" PIECE OF YARN
OR STRING THROUGH
EACH HOLE (AS
INDICATED BY
BROKEN LINES) SO
JULIE JELLYFISH
RESEMBLES
MRS. JELLYFISH.

EYE PATTERN
FOR JULIE
JELLYFISH—
WHITE PAPER

JELLY BEAN JAR LID—
PLACE OVER JAR TOP.

JELLY BEAN JAR—
CUT OUT JAR SHAPE
AND CUT ALONG
INSIDE BROKEN LINE
TO MAKE JAR OUTLINE.

J

The Kangaroo and the Keys

Once upon a time, there was a kangaroo named Kerry who carried the key to her house on a ribbon around her neck. When Kerry hopped home from school, her parents, Mr. and Mrs. Kangaroo were still at work. So everyday, Kerry used her shiny key to unlock the door and let herself into the house. Once inside her house, she carefully closed and locked the door again until her parents came home.

Kerry was a careful kangaroo. Each morning before school, she would take the key off the hook in the kitchen and hang it safely around her neck. Each afternoon after school, she would replace the key on the hook again. Kerry made sure the key was always in the correct spot. That is, until one day last week...

On that particular morning, Kerry took the key off the hook and hung the ribbon around her neck. She then hopped off to school.

At school, she read a book about kites, played kickball with her friend Kenny Kangaroo, and ate kidney pie for lunch. Back at her desk, she printed neat rows of the letter "K" until the clock struck three.

After school, she hopped home with Kenny whose house was down the street. They were almost home when Kerry stopped hopping. *"I can't find my key!"* she cried. *"I lost my key!"*

Kenny Kangaroo tried to help. *"Don't worry, Kerry,"* he said. *"We'll look everywhere. We'll find it!"*

They looked everywhere for the key, but by the time it was dark, they knew they had to hop home. Kenny felt sorry for Kerry and Kerry felt sorry for herself.

By the time they got home, Kerry's parents were in the kitchen. *"We were worried,"* they said. *"Where were you, Kerry?"*

"I did hop straight home from school," began Kerry, *"but then I couldn't get in the house..."*

"Why not?" interrupted Mrs. Kangaroo. *"You have your key right there in your pouch. I can see the ribbon peeking out."* And, sure enough, the ribbon and the key had fallen into Kerry's pouch--the only place she had forgotten to look!

KIDNEY PIE

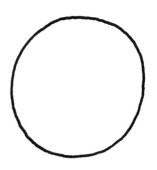

KICKBALL-
ORANGE FELT

PAPER WITH "K's"

BOOK ABOUT KITES

Comprehension Questions

• Why did Kerry Kangaroo have a key to her house? Where did she keep her key?
• What did Kerry and Kenny do at school? What do you do at school?
• How did Kerry feel when she lost the key?
• Where did Kerry find her key? Where will Kerry keep her key from now on?

Follow-up Activities

Unlock Imagination

On a novelty key ring, place some old keys and give these keys to your children to play with. Keys are a very grown-up looking accessory; they will become a treasured, sought after toy.

Find Key Reasons

Have your children help you make a list of all the places they know that can be locked with a key. Discuss why keys might be helpful to people. Go on a lock hunt to find locks in your building or neighborhood.

Read About Pocket Animals

Ask your librarian for books and pictures on pouched mammals called marsupials. Most of these animals, including the koala and the kangaroo, live in Australia.

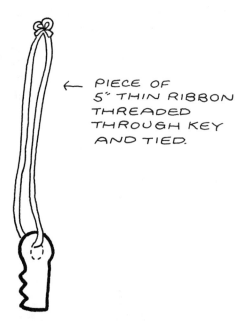

← PIECE OF 5" THIN RIBBON THREADED THROUGH KEY AND TIED.

KEY FOR KERRY KANGAROO— GREY FELT; CUT HOLE AROUND BROKEN LINE.

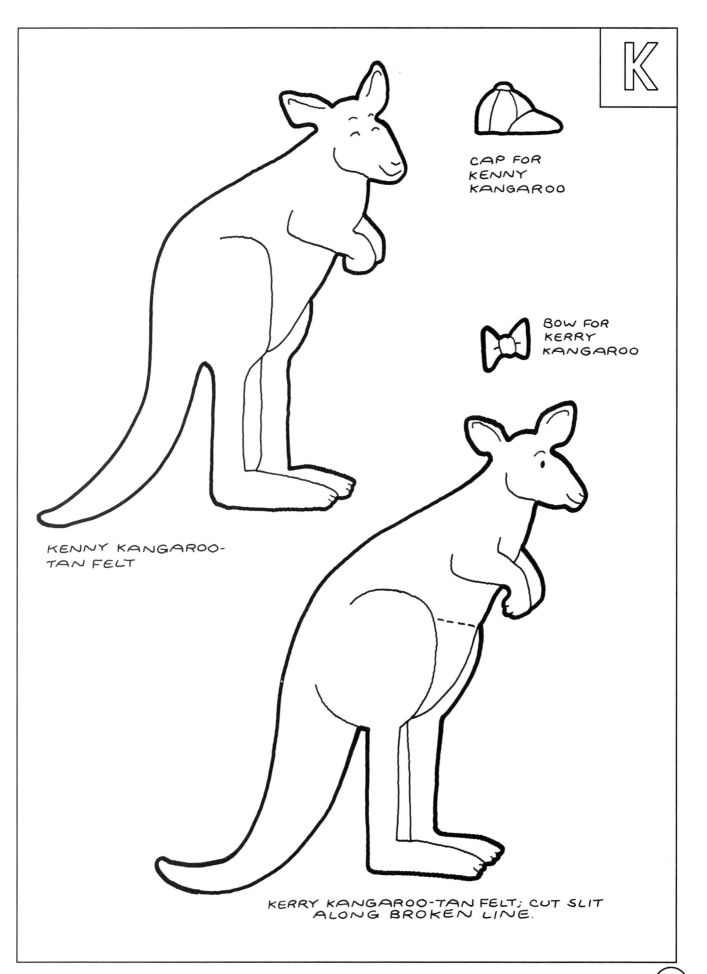

CAP FOR
KENNY
KANGAROO

BOW FOR
KERRY
KANGAROO

KENNY KANGAROO-
TAN FELT

KERRY KANGAROO-TAN FELT; CUT SLIT
ALONG BROKEN LINE.

K

HAT FOR
MR. KANGAROO

HAT FOR
MRS. KANGAROO

MR. KANGAROO-
TAN FELT

MRS. KANGAROO-TAN FELT

The Lion and the Lamb

Once upon a time, a lamb wandered away from her flock and was lost. By and by, she wandered near a cave. Now, in the cave lived a fierce and horrible lion. When he saw the tired, hungry lamb enter his cave, the lion said in a sweet voice, *"Come here, little lamb, I will not hurt you. I want to help you."*

The lamb was usually afraid of lions; but this lion seemed so friendly that she decided to trust him. She walked a bit farther into the cave.

"Come, help me finish my delicious supper," offered the lion. *"Then, you can rest on this bed of leaves."*

The lamb felt a little nervous, but she walked over to the lion and began to share his juicy meal. When she was full, the lamb laid down next to the lion and fell asleep.

Now the lion was *not* to be trusted. He planned on feeding the lamb plenty of food so that she would grow plump and fat; and then, he was going to eat her up.

LEMONADE-
YELLOW FELT

Everyday, the lamb grew fatter. She was so grateful to the lion, that she did him lovely favors. She mailed his letters, she made him lemonade, and she gathered extra leaves for his bed. Day by day, the lion and the lamb lived quite nicely together.

Soon, the lion knew that the lamb was fat enough to eat. He built a fire from long logs and, when the flames were high and hot, he called the lamb to come over. *"Look at my log fire, Lamb,"* he said. *"Put your leg over it and see if it is hot enough to cook dinner on?"*

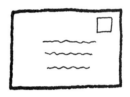

LETTER

The lamb stood next to the fire and held out her little leg over the flames. The lion stood behind her ready to push her in. One, two, three... The lion took a deep breath, closed his eyes, and realized that he couldn't kill the lamb. He knew that if he ate her, his tummy would be full, but his heart would be empty.

After that day, the lion and the lamb became better friends than ever. The lamb was never again lonesome or lost, and the lion's heart was forever full.

LEAF

Comprehension Questions

• Why did the lamb get lost? Why did the lamb trust the lion?
• What was the lion's plan for the lamb? What did he do to help make the lamb taste delicious?
• Did the lion eat the lamb? Why not?
• How did the lion change in the story? Would you rather be the lion or the lamb?

Follow-up Activities

Nibble Lamb and Lion Snacks

Use round crackers or party breads for faces. Have children spread with cream cheese for the lamb, and peanut butter for the lion. Have them sprinkle on coconut for the lamb, and grated carrots for the lion's mane. Facial features may be added with raisins or nuts. Serve with lemonade.

Play "Lamb, Lamb, Lion"

Have children sit in circle. Choose one child to be the lamb. She walks around the circle tapping children on head while repeating, *"lamb--lamb--lamb..."* until she says, *"lion."* The chosen lion then chases the lamb around the circle to her safe home spot. The lion then becomes the next lamb.

Get Lost

Role play with the children possible scenarios where they could find themselves lost. Offer safe solutions and positive choices they can make when faced with this scary dilemma.

LEAF BED - GREEN FELT

LOGS FOR FIRE-
BROWN FELT

EYE PATTERN
FOR LION-
WHITE PAPER

LION-TAN FELT
FOR "MANE"-COLOR
IN DARK BROWN
OR GLUE PIECES OF
YARN ALL AROUND.

L

LAMB- PINK FELT

FOR "WOOL": CUT "WOOL" SHAPE (BELOW) OUT OF WHITE
FELT AND GLUE ONTO LAMB'S BODY
OR GLUE COTTON BALLS OR PADS ONTO
BODY.

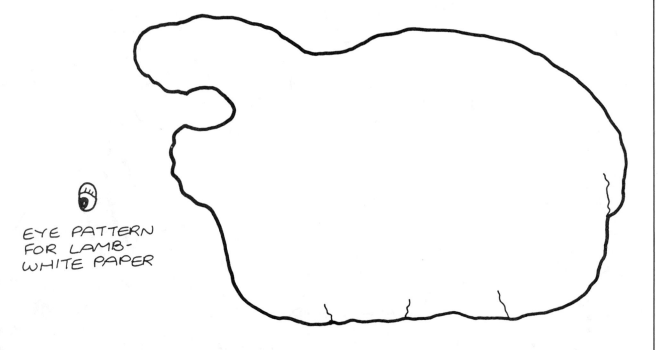

EYE PATTERN
FOR LAMB-
WHITE PAPER

The Marvelous Magical Mandolin

Once upon a time, there was a merry magician who was also very musical. He especially loved the beautiful music that came from his magical mandolin.

The magical mandolin had six strings. To get the mandolin to play, the merry magician would pick the instrument up and gently strum the strings three times. The mandolin would then play the sweetest, prettiest music in all the land. When it was time for the music to end, the merry magician would once again pick the instrument up and gently strum the strings three times. The mandolin would then be very calm and quiet.

Whenever the music played, mockingbirds came to the magician's window pane to chirp and sing.

Nearby, there lived a mean monster who thought of no one but himself. He lived all alone in a mansion high up on a mountain. He had heard of the marvelous mandolin and he had even paid money to see it play.

"I want that instrument," thought the mean monster to himself. *" I will have to steal it to make it mine!"*

With a magic spell, he turned himself into a meek mouse and crept into the home of the merry magician. He grabbed the mandolin and made off with it in his mouth!

Back home, at his mansion on the mountain, the monster tried to make the magical mandolin play some of its marvelous music. The monster remembered how the magician had strummed the mandolin gently three times, and he copied what he remembered. The mandolin remained very calm and quiet. The monster tried again, a little harder this time. Still, the mandolin was calm and quiet. Finally, the monster strummed the mandolin as hard as he could, but it was no use.

What the monster didn't know was that the mandolin would only play for mild and merry people. The mandolin would not play for the monster who was so mean, so the monster threw the mandolin out the window. It landed at the foot of the mountain.

Meanwhile, the merry magician was very melancholy to discover that his mandolin was missing. The mockingbirds who came to sing were also sad to discover that the mandolin was missing. They promised to help get it back.

When the merry magician had just about given up hope, the mockingbirds flew to the window with the magical mandolin.

"We heard its music coming from the foot of the mountain," the mockingbirds explained, *"and we followed it. The monster had stolen the mandolin from you, but the mandolin wouldn't play for him. We have returned it safely home."*

And in celebration, beneath the light of the moon, the magician and the mockingbirds danced together to the music of the magical mandolin.

MOON

MANDOLIN
MUSICAL
NOTES

Comprehension Questions

• What did the merry magician have that was so special? Have you ever seen a mandolin? Have you ever seen a guitar? (The guitar and the mandolin are closely related instruments.) How is a mandolin played?

• Why did the monster want the magical mandolin? How did he try to get it from the merry magician? Why wouldn't the mandolin play for the monster?

• Who helped the merry magician get the mandolin back again? What will the mean monster do now?

• Do we have any instruments at school? How do they make music?

Follow-up Activities

Look at a Mandolin

Find pictures of mandolins and other stringed instruments in your library. Encourage children to take a closer look at the stringed instruments the next time they see a folksinger perform or attend an instrumental concert.

Visit a Magic Shop

Find out more about magic and magicians by visiting a local magic shop. (Call ahead to be certain that the shop will welcome a group of children. Some shops will put on small demonstrations for young people, and there are always a variety of very inexpensive tricks available for purchase.)

Make Money Rubbings

Place a variety of coins under lightweight sheets of typing paper. (Secure coins to table with tiny bits of clay.) Place a crayon on its side and rub until coin relief appears. Help children to identify the types of coins in the rubbings and encourage them to count how many coins appear. If amounts are kept low, older children may be able to add up the total amount of money that appears on the paper.

MOCKINGBIRD-
GREY FELT

MOUSE-
GREY
FELT

MAGICIAN-
DRAW IN DETAILS

MAGICIAN'S
CAPE- PLACE
CAPE BEHIND
MAGICIAN
AND GLUE ONTO
MAGICIAN AT
SHOULDERS AND
BACK, LEAVING
HAND FREE TO
"STRUM" THE
MANDOLIN

MANDOLIN

① CUT MANDOLIN SHAPE
   FROM BROWN FELT.

② CUT A 33" LENGTH OF
   THREAD AND THREAD IT
   THROUGH NEEDLE.

③ ON MANDOLIN-SEW
   BACK AND FORTH 6
   6 TIMES TO MAKE
   6 3" STRINGS

MONSTER'S EYES-
WHITE PAPER

MONSTER'S TEETH-
WHITE FELT OR PAPER

MONSTER'S
SHORTS-
BRIGHT FELT
OR FABRIC

MONSTER-
LIME GREEN FELT

MANSION ON
A MOUNTAIN-
WHITE FELT;
DRAW IN
DETAILS AND
COLOR IN
"ROCKY" PART
OF MOUNTAIN
(BROWN OR GREY)

Noodlehead and Needlenose (N)

Once upon a time, there were two sillies named Noodlehead and Needlenose.

One day, Noodlehead's mother wanted him to go to the store for her. *"Here are nine pennies,"* she said to Noodlehead. *"I want nine nails from the store. Please go right down the road and through the woods to the store and back again. I need the nails to build a fence for my vegetable garden, so don't you be gone long."*

So Noodlehead took the nine pennies, tucked them into his pocket, and started down the road. On his way to the store, he came upon his friend Needlenose.

"Hi, Noodlehead!" said Needlenose. *"Where are you going?"*

"Hi, Needlenose. I'm going right down the road and through the woods to the store for my mother. She gave me nine pennies to buy nine nails to help build a fence for her vegetable garden."

"I'll trade you these nine magic nuts for your nine pennies," said Needlenose. And he pulled nine nuts out from his pocket.

"Oh, maybe I shouldn't do that," said Noodlehead. *"My mother told me to go right down the road, and through the woods to the store, and back. She might be mad if I don't do what she says."*

"Before you know it," said Needlenose, *"you'll be rich. You'll be just like the boy named Jack who traded his mother's cow for three beans. The beans grew overnight and Jack climbed the beanstalk to capture the giant's gold!"*

"Wow!" said Noodlehead. *"Jack was lucky! Will these nuts grow like that?"*

"No," said Needlenose, *"but these nuts will teach you something very magical, indeed!"*

So Noodlehead traded the nine pennies for the nuts. He went back home to his mother without the nine pennies and without the nine nails. His mother was so angry, that she spanked Noodlehead and sent him to bed. Noodlehead threw the nuts out the window. There they lay until the squirrel family ate them. Without the fence, the animals ate all of the vegetables in the garden too, so Noodlehead and his mother had to eat noodles for the rest of the winter.

"I hope you've learned a lesson from all of this," said Noodlehead's mother.

"I sure have," said Noodlehead. *"The next time I'm asked to trade away my pennies, I'll make sure that I trade for beans from a boy named Jack, not nuts from a boy named Needlenose!"*

MOCKINGBIRD-
GREY FELT

MOUSE-
GREY FELT

Comprehension Questions

• What did Noodlehead's mother need from the store? How much money did she give him?

• Who did Noodlehead meet on the way to the store? What did Needlenose want to trade for the pennies?

• What happened when Noodlehead traded his pennies for the nuts?

• Do you think Noodlehead should have traded away his pennies? What will Noodlehead do next time?

Follow-up Activities

Nibble Noodles

Share a variety of noodles with your group. Discuss the color and texture of noodles before and after cooking. For toppings, offer tomato sauce, butter, and grated cheeses.

Make Nines

Gather nine children together and proceed to separate children into two sets creating a variety of addition combinations. See how many combinations your group can create.

Review Rules

In the story, Noodlehead gets into trouble because he doesn't follow his mother's instructions. Discuss with your group rules they have to follow in school and at home. Also, discuss reasons for the rules, as well as possible consequences that may result if important rules are not followed.

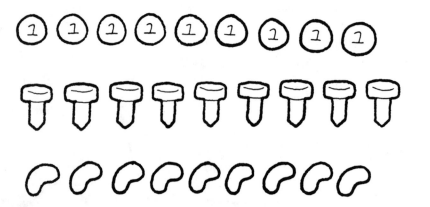

NINE PENNIES-
BROWN FELT

NINE NAILS-
GREY FELT

NINE NUTS-
TAN FELT

NOODLEHEAD-COLOR IN HAIR
OR GLUE ON PIECES OF YARN
FOR HAIR

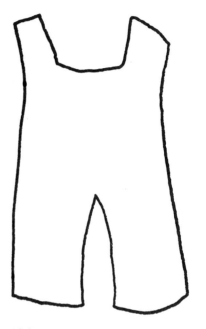

NOODLEHEAD'S OVERALLS-
ADD POCKET

POCKET FOR OVERALLS-
CUT 1 FOR NOODLEHEAD'S
AND 2 FOR NEEDLENOSE'S
OVERALLS- STITCH ON
AROUND 3 SIDES AS INDICATED

EYE PATTERN FOR NOODLEHEAD (CUT 2),
NOODLEHEAD'S MOTHER (CUT 2), AND
NEEDLENOSE (CUT 1)- TOTAL 5- WHITE
PAPER

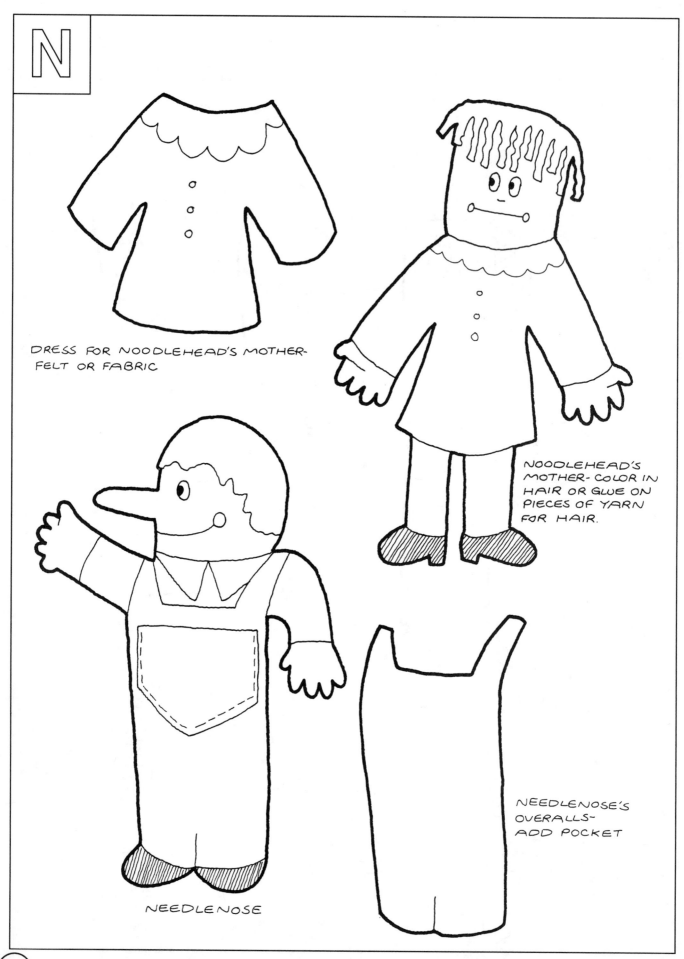

N

DRESS FOR NOODLEHEAD'S MOTHER-
FELT OR FABRIC

NOODLEHEAD'S
MOTHER- COLOR IN
HAIR OR GLUE ON
PIECES OF YARN
FOR HAIR.

NEEDLENOSE'S
OVERALLS-
ADD POCKET

NEEDLENOSE

The Octopus and the Olive

Once upon a time, Octopus planned a dinner party for her friends. She had cooked delicious omelets, and wanted to serve them with some olives that she had been saving just for this occasion. She had placed the olive jar up high on a shelf over the oven.

"Oh, my!" said Octopus when she saw how high up the jar of olives were. *"How will I ever reach them? I want to serve them to my dinner guests."* She then stood on her tippy-toes and stretched to reach the jar or olives, but it was no use.

Just then there was a knock at the door. It was Otter. *"Hello, Octopus,"* said Otter. *"What are you doing?"*

"Hello, Otter," said Octopus. *"I'm trying to reach the olive jar high up on the shelf over the oven. I want to serve them to my dinner guests."*

"I have an idea," said Otter. *"I will stand on top of you and, together, we will be able to reach the jar of olives!"* So, Otter climbed on Octopus' back. Together they stood on tippy-toes, and, together, they *stretched* to reach the jar of olives, but it was no use.

Just then, there was a knock at the door. It was Ostrich. *"Hello, Octopus and Otter,"* said Ostrich. *"What are you doing?"*

"Hello, Ostrich," said Octopus. *"We're trying to reach the olive jar high up on the shelf over the oven. I want to serve them to my dinner guests."*

"I have an idea," said Ostrich. *"I will stand on top of you both. All together we will be able to reach the jar of olives!"*

So, Ostrich climbed on top of Otter who was on top of Octopus. Together, they all stood on tippy-toes, and together they *stretched* to reach the jar of olives, but it was no use.

Just then, there was a knock at the door. It was Osprey. *"Hello, Octopus, Otter, and Ostrich. What are you doing? Don't just stand there playing on top of each other. I'm hungry for Octopus' omelet tonight. And, I see a jar of olives that would be tasty, too."*

Suddenly, with just two flaps of his strong hawk wings, he flew up to the jar of olives on the shelf over the oven, and brought it down to Octopus.

Octopus looked at Otter; Otter looked at Ostrich; Ostrich looked at Octopus. And, they all looked at the olives. *"Let's eat!"* said the Osprey.

And they did.

Comprehension Questions

• What did Octopus want to serve for dinner? Whom did she invite for dinner?

• What did Octopus do by herself to reach the jar of olives? What idea did Otter have?

• Who came to Octopus' house after Otter? What was Ostrich's idea for getting the olives?

• How did Osprey help? What did Osprey think the animals were doing? How did the animals feel when Osprey got the olives?

Follow-up Activities

Experiment With Olives

Share green and black olives with your children. Make a bar graph showing olive preferences (green, black, none). If olives are a popular food, mix them in egg salad or whip up an over-sized egg and olive omelet.

Play "On Top"

Have ready a collection of small wooden cubes. Have children take turns placing one cube on top of another to build a tower. Try each day to see how high you can cooperatively build. Aim for higher towers. Use a wall chart to keep track of your progress.

Reinforce the Letter O

Stick paper reinforcers randomly on colored paper and provide the children with crayons and markers to generate op-art designs around the O-shapes! Or, suggest that the children use the reinforcers to create realistic-looking O-art of their own-- centers of flowers, wheels on a truck, eyes on a face.

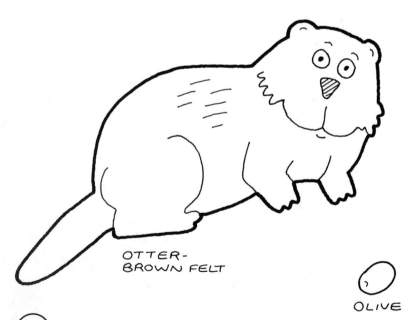

OTTER- BROWN FELT

OLIVE

JAR OF OLIVES- WHITE FELT

DRAW IN OLIVES-OR- CUT OLIVE SHAPES OUT OF OLIVE GREEN FELT AND GLUE ONTO THE JAR.

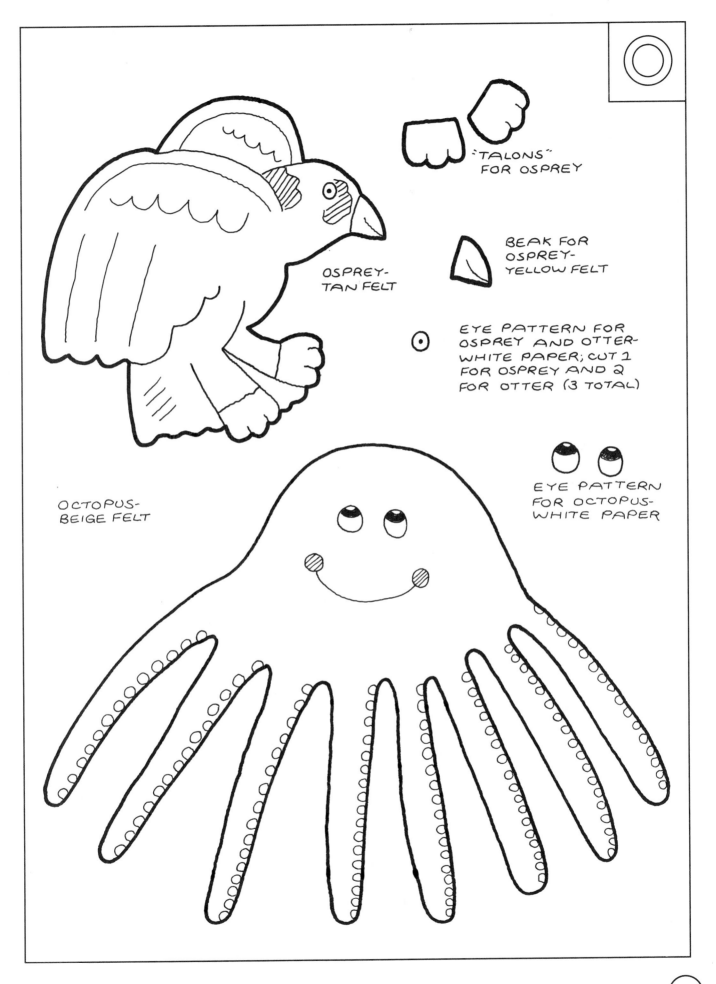

"TALONS"
FOR OSPREY

BEAK FOR
OSPREY-
YELLOW FELT

EYE PATTERN FOR
OSPREY AND OTTER-
WHITE PAPER; CUT 1
FOR OSPREY AND 2
FOR OTTER (3 TOTAL)

OSPREY-
TAN FELT

EYE PATTERN
FOR OCTOPUS-
WHITE PAPER

OCTOPUS-
BEIGE FELT

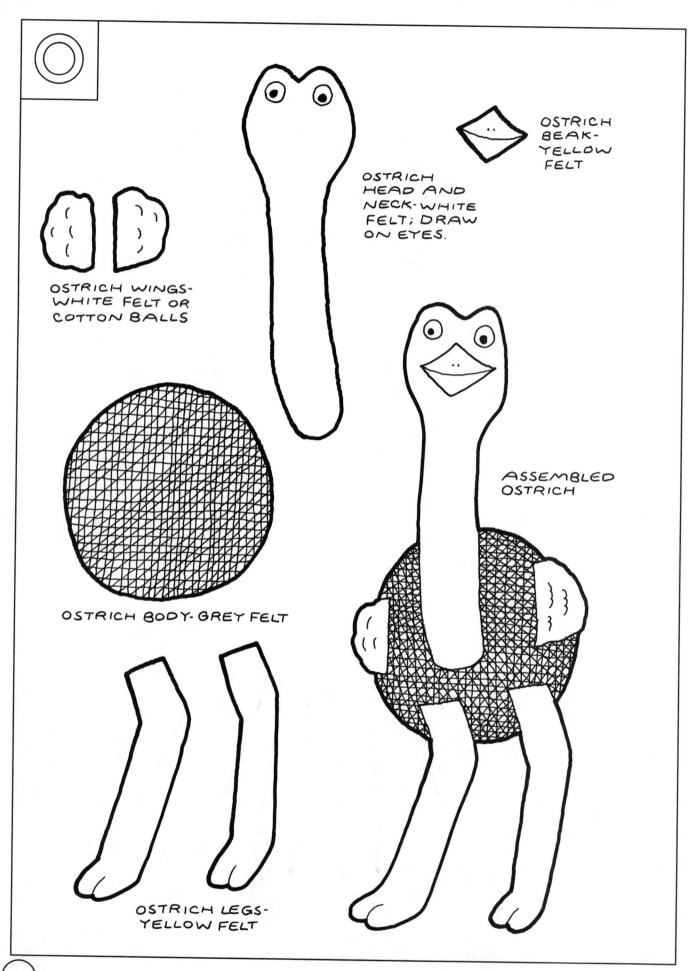

OSTRICH BEAK-
YELLOW
FELT

OSTRICH
HEAD AND
NECK-WHITE
FELT; DRAW
ON EYES.

OSTRICH WINGS-
WHITE FELT OR
COTTON BALLS

ASSEMBLED
OSTRICH

OSTRICH BODY-GREY FELT

OSTRICH LEGS-
YELLOW FELT

80

The Pig Who Wouldn't Pick Up

Once upon a time, there lived together a pair of pigs named Pete and Penny. Now Pete and Penny were pleasant pigs who almost always enjoyed being partners in work and play. When it was time for Pete to pop a pot of popcorn, Penny pitched in and helped. When it was time for Penny to plant petunias, Pete pitched in and helped. And when it was time for them both to paint the fence around the pigpen pink, they pitched in and helped each other. When they were done, they shared a picnic together at the playground.

Yes, Pete and Penny were a very special pair of pigs who shared a lot together. Still, there was one thing they couldn't agree upon. Pete was a particularly neat pig, while Penny was a particularly messy pig. While Penny was busy messing up the pigpen, Pete was busy cleaning it. Everyday he would clean, clean, clean, and everyday she would mess, mess, mess. Every night he would pick up-up-up, and every night, she would put down-down-down the same piggy mess.

Finally, Pete thought he had an idea to help solve the problem. *"Why don't we split the pigpen into two equal parts,"* he suggested. *"You may keep your half messy, play messy games, and I'll keep my half neat."* It sounded like a good idea to Penny, so it was settled.

At first, Penny liked having one part of the pigpen to herself. She never put anything away. She left out paints and paint brushes, pickles, and peanut butter. She left out pears and pants, pies, and peanuts. Pretty soon, she had a mile-high piggy pile of mess, and Pete Pig did not tell her when to clean it up. Pretty soon, however, the pile became so high, that Penny couldn't find her plaid party dress or her precious book of pig poetry that her Aunt Patty Pig had given to her. Penny Pig soon began to pout.

At first, Pete Pig liked having one part of the pigpen to himself. His part of the pen was perfect and pretty. His pants and playthings were piled in neat little piles and his piggy messes were thrown into a pail for the trash. Pretty soon, however, Pete Pig found that he didn't have much to do. After plumping his pillows and polishing his piano, Pete Pig was done with his work. He wanted to play, but Penny Pig was too busy looking through her pile to play with him. Pete Pig soon began to pout.

Pete Pig had another idea. *"Let me clean your part of the pigpen,"* he said *"and I'll play any messy game you want to play."* So Pete cleaned Penny's part of the pen, and then he played with her in some messy puddles of mud, and neither pig had to ever pout again.

PLAYTHINGS

PICKLE

PEANUT BUTTER

POPCORN (TO PUT INTO POT)- YELLOW FELT

POT

Comprehension Questions

• What kind of a pig was Penny Pig? What kind of a pig was Pete Pig? How were they the same? How were they different?
• What were some of the things that were in the pigpen.
• If you were Pete Pig, would you have cleaned up Penny's side of the pigpen?

Follow-up Activities

Play a Pigpen Memory Game

Paint a box pink and tell the children that this box is a pigpen. Into the pigpen, place articles that begin with the sound of the letter "P"--a pencil, a pen, a pepper, paper, paint, paint brush. Allow the group to peek at the pigpen for a predetermined length of time (one or two minutes). Hide the pigpen and ask the children to recall what was in the pigpen by drawing the contents on paper.

"Think Pink" Paintings

Have the children mix various amounts of red and white paint to create a multitude of pink hues. Place these homemade concoctions in the easel and watch for the pink creations that emerge.

**Piggy Pictures
(Before and After)**

Take photographs of classroom messes (including the teacher's desk!) and then photograph these same spots after the kiddy clean-up crew has been through. Compare the before and after shots on a large piece of oaktag and have the children dictate funny captions for the pictures. Beside the photographic display, hang a language experience chart of child-dictated clean-up hints and how-to's.

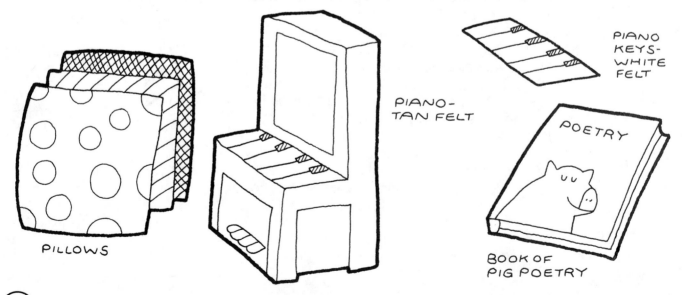

PILLOWS

PIANO-
TAN FELT

PIANO
KEYS-
WHITE
FELT

POETRY

BOOK OF
PIG POETRY

OPTIONAL:
PIPE
CLEANER
TAIL

PETE PIG- PINK FELT

PAINT BRUSH

PETUNIA

OPTIONAL:
PIPE
CLEANER
TAIL

EYE PATTERN
FOR PENNY
AND PETE PIG-
CUT 1 FOR BOTH
(TOTAL 2)-
WHITE PAPER

PENNY PIG- PINK FELT WITH
DRAWN ON MUD SPOTS

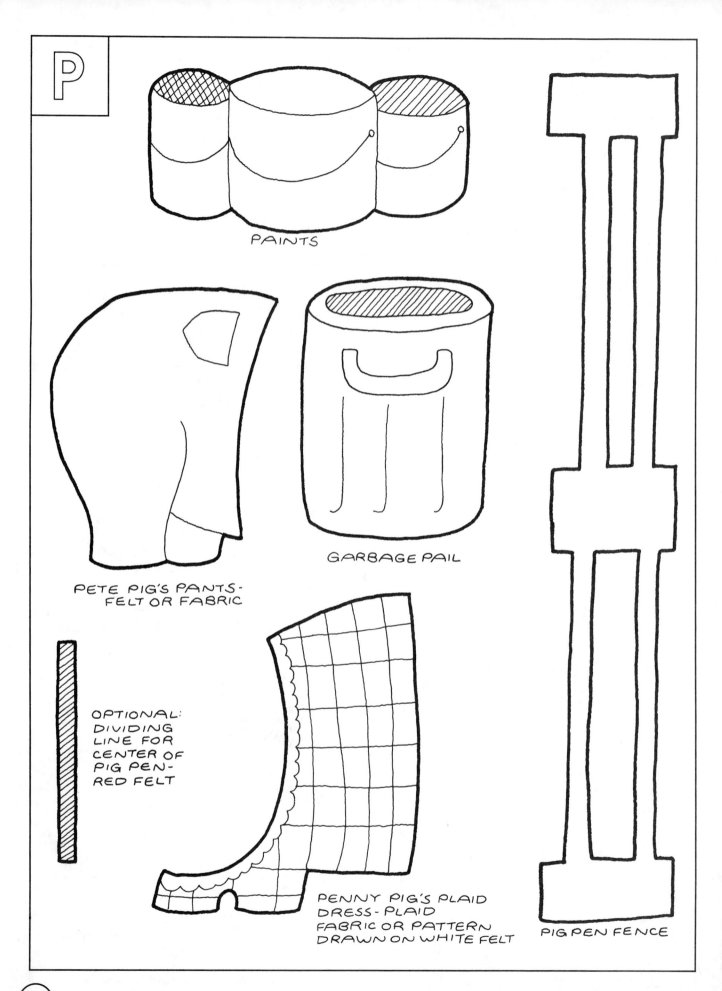

P

PAINTS

PETE PIG'S PANTS-
FELT OR FABRIC

GARBAGE PAIL

OPTIONAL:
DIVIDING
LINE FOR
CENTER OF
PIG PEN-
RED FELT

PENNY PIG'S PLAID
DRESS- PLAID
FABRIC OR PATTERN
DRAWN ON WHITE FELT

PIG PEN FENCE

The Queen's Quilt

Once upon a time, there was a queen who loved to sleep, but had trouble staying warm in bed. She tried wearing a pair of warm pajamas to bed, but she still shivered and quivered with the cold. She tried wearing warm socks to cover her royal toes in bed, but she still shivered and quivered from the cold. She even tried wearing a warm wooly nightcap to bed, but *still* she shivered and quivered from the cold! It was clearly a queen-sized problem.

The queen thought and thought. She decided that she probably needed a new royal quilt; so, she told her royal quilters about her problem. While the quilters all agreed that a new quilt would help the Queen quit quivering, they couldn't agree on how to make the quilt, and they began to fight and quarrel. The first quilter wanted to sew a red quilt; the second quilter wanted to sew a yellow quilt; the third quilter wanted to sew a green quilt; and the fourth quilter wanted to sew a blue quilt.

The wise queen solved the problem. She told each of her four royal quilters to quilt *one quarter* of the whole quilt in the color they liked best.

When they were done, they brought her the four pieces or four quarters that they had quilted, and the queen sewed them all together into one whole quilt. The royal quilters thought that this patchwork quilt looked rather queer, but the queen thought it looked quite quaint, and she was never shivery or quivery again.

NIGHT CAP
FOR QUEEN

SOCKS FOR
QUEEN

CROWN FOR
QUEEN

Comprehension Questions

• Why do you think the queen was always chilly in bed ?
• How did the queen solve her problem? Have you ever seen a real quilt? How is a quilt the same as a blanket? How is it different? How does a quilt or a blanket help someone stay warm?
• What happens to our bodies when we're too cold? too hot?

Follow-up Activities

Plan a Paper Quilt

Show children a real quilt or pictures of quilt design. Then, provide each child with a plain piece of paper that has been folded into four quarters. Children draw theme pictures in each of the quarters--favorite things, family members, animals, friends. The quilt pieces are then joined on a larger length of paper to represent a quilt. Yarn stitches and fringe will help the paper quilt appear more authentic.

Make a "Hot and Cold Book"

Discuss things that are hot and things that are cold. Show children that some colors are "warm" (red, orange, brown) and some are "cool" (blue, green). Staple red and blue paper together in booklets for the children to decorate with hot and cold pictures.

Forage for Fourths

Look for things that come in sets of four--animal legs, window panes, coat buttons, car tires. Begin a list and continue to add to it as discoveries are made throughout the year.

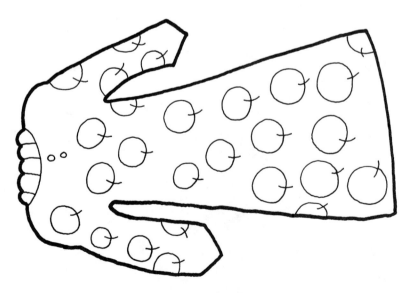

PAJAMAS FOR QUEEN--DECORATE WITH "Q'S."

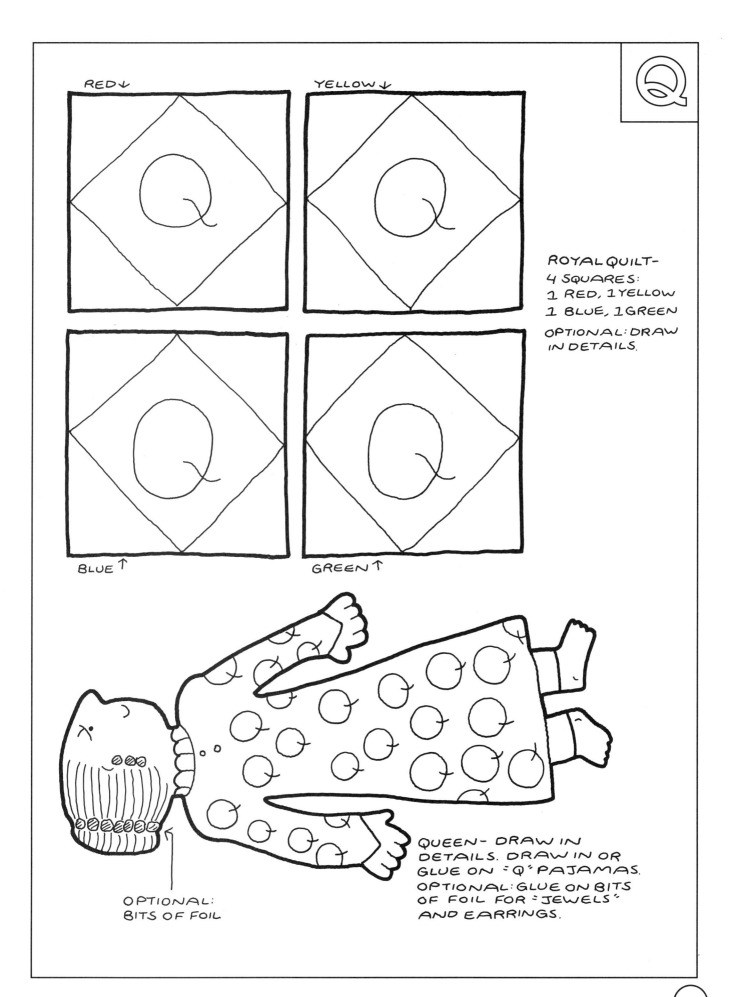

RED↓

YELLOW↓

BLUE↑

GREEN↑

ROYAL QUILT—
4 SQUARES:
1 RED, 1 YELLOW
1 BLUE, 1 GREEN

OPTIONAL: DRAW
IN DETAILS.

OPTIONAL:
BITS OF FOIL

QUEEN— DRAW IN
DETAILS. DRAW IN OR
GLUE ON "Q" PAJAMAS.
OPTIONAL: GLUE ON BITS
OF FOIL FOR "JEWELS"
AND EARRINGS.

Q

4 QUILTERS-
WHITE OR TAN
FELT; GLUE
ON YARN
FOR BEARDS
AND DRAW
IN DETAILS.

The Racoons and the Rainbow

Once upon a time, two little raccoons were washing their paws in a river. All at once, a big, black rain cloud appeared; the two raccoons scampered under a tree and perched on the roots to keep dry.

As soon as the storm had passed, the two raccoons came out from under the tree just in time to see a beautiful rainbow stretched across the sky.

"Ooooh," said the raccoons together. *"Let's follow it and find the riches at the end."* Of course, those raccoons had heard that waiting at the end of the rainbow is a pot of riches for whom ever can find it. So, off they went, running along the bank of the river to find the end of the rainbow.

They had not gone very far, when they saw something shining in the river water. They bent closer and saw a pile of sparkling red rock jewels. The raccoons scooped up as many red rocks as their little paws could hold, but all those rocks were too heavy and slippery to carry to the end of the rainbow, so each raccoon chose one red rock to keep.

RED
ROCKS-
RED FELT

After the raccoons collected their rocks, they realized that they were hungry. They began to look for food and soon found a raspberry bush full of ripe, juicy raspberries. The little raccoons ate and ate and ate. They ate until their tummies were plump and round with raspberries, and then they raced each other to a rosebush near the river. They were having so much fun that they almost ran over Mr. Rabbit who was just crawling out of his hole.

"Where are you two going?" said the wise old rabbit. *"Don't you know it's almost bedtime?"*

"We're trying to find the end of the rainbow," said the raccoons. *"We're going to capture the riches there."*

"What have you done during your journey to the rainbow's end?" said the rabbit.

"We found the red sparkle rocks, we ate ripe raspberries , and we raced to a rosebush," said the raccoons.

"And did you have fun together?" asked the rabbit.

"Oh, we always have fun together. We're best friends," answered the raccoons.

"Then, in each other's friendship, you have discovered treasures far more precious than the rainbow's riches. Run home, little raccoons, and remember that the most special riches are never kept in a pot at the rainbow's end, but rather are stored deep in your heart!"

And so, the two little raccoons headed back home--red sparkle rocks clutched in their paws, and the rich memory of a happy day locked in their hearts.

Comprehension Questions

• Where did the two little raccoons live? How did the weather change in the beginning of the story? Why did the raccoons sit on the roots of the tree?

• What appeared in the sky after the storm? Have you ever seen a rainbow? What did it look like?

• What did the raccoons do on their way to the end of the rainbow?

• What other animal did the raccoons meet on their journey? What did the rabbit mean when he said that *"the best treasure is stored in your heart?"*

Follow-up Activities

Fantasize about the Rainbow's Riches

Have the children hypothesize and then illustrate what might be found at the end of the rainbow. Print their dictated descriptions below the pictures. Create a bulletin-board display entitled, "Discovering Rainbow Riches."

Race Raccoons

Using the flannelboard raccoon pattern, cut raccoon shapes from lightweight paper or cellophane. Place raccoons on smooth surface (floor or table). Indicate a finish line, and have children take turns pushing raccoons to finish by blowing on them through a clean straw. (Do not share straws.) Discuss the effect of moving air (wind) on objects.

Enjoy Raspberries

Offer your children a sample of real, ripe raspberries. Before tasting, discuss the color and composition of this intricate fruit. Also discuss other food products that utilize raspberries--jams, jellies, cookies, ice cream.

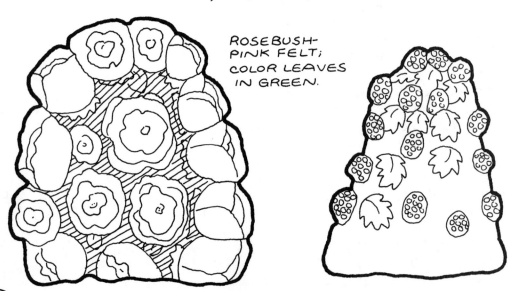

ROSEBUSH-
PINK FELT;
COLOR LEAVES
IN GREEN.

RASPBERRY-
RED FELT

RASPBERRY
BUSH - GREEN
FELT; COLOR
RASPBERRIES
IN RED OR
GLUE ON
RED FELT
RASPBERRIES

2 RACCOONS- TAN FELT; DRAW DETAILS IN BLACK

EYE PATTERN FOR
RACCOONS- WHITE
PAPER; CUT 2 FOR
BOTH RACCOONS
(4 TOTAL)

WISE OLD RABBIT-
OPTIONAL: GLUE ON
COTTON BALL FOR
TAIL AND STRING
FOR WHISKERS

RIVER

R

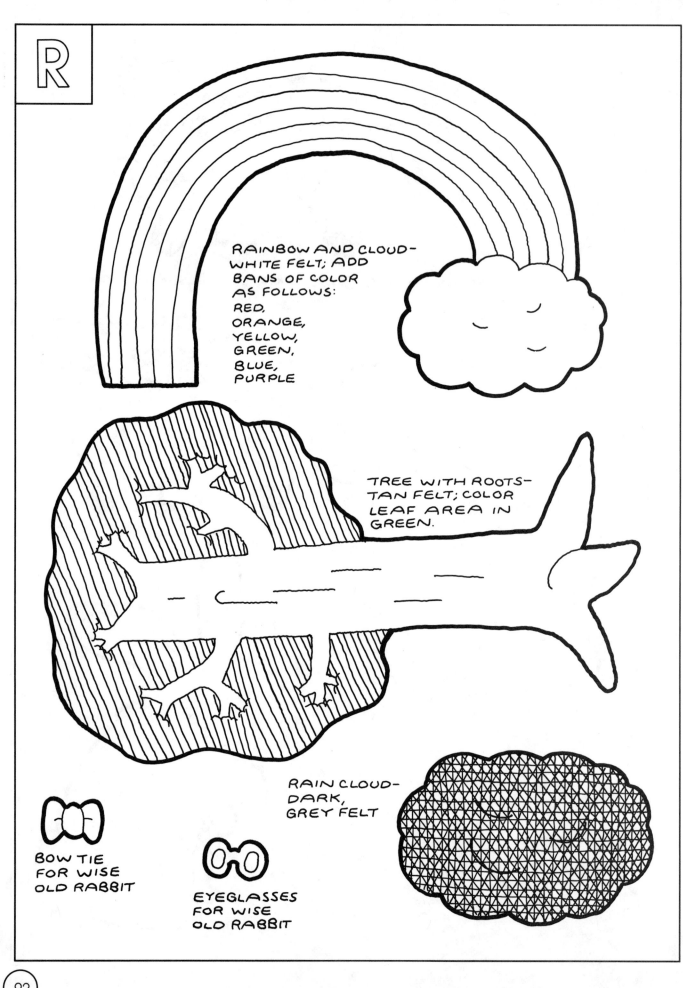

R

RAINBOW AND CLOUD-
WHITE FELT; ADD
BANS OF COLOR
AS FOLLOWS:
RED,
ORANGE,
YELLOW,
GREEN,
BLUE,
PURPLE

TREE WITH ROOTS-
TAN FELT; COLOR
LEAF AREA IN
GREEN.

BOW TIE
FOR WISE
OLD RABBIT

EYEGLASSES
FOR WISE
OLD RABBIT

RAIN CLOUD-
DARK,
GREY FELT

Sara Snake Tries to Seesaw

Once upon a time, there was a little snake named Sara who loved to watch the children on the playground near school.

One day, when Sara saw the children swinging on the swings, sliding on the slide, and soaring up and down on the seesaw, she thought, *"I want to try those things, too."*

So, when all of the children had gone home for supper, Sara slithered on to the playground. She had a super time swinging on the swing and sliding down the slide, but more than anything else, she wanted to soar up and down on the seesaw.

She slithered over to it and sat on the seat at the low end. She held onto the handle and waited for the seesaw to ride up and down. But nothing happened.

Sara thought to herself, *"Maybe this side of the seesaw is stuck. I'll slither over and try the other side that is up in the air."* So Sara slithered to the middle of the slide and slowly headed toward the side that was up in the air. She sat on the seat, held onto the handle and waited for the seesaw to ride up and down. But, nothing happened. And, to make matters worse, Sara was once again sitting on the low end of the seesaw.

Just then, Steve Snake slithered by. *"Hi, Sara,"* he called. *"What's up?"*

"I'd like to be up," said Sara, *"up in the air on this seesaw, but whenever I sit on the seat, nothing happens. The children make it go up and down all the time!"*

"I bet I can save the day," said Steve. And with that, he picked up a large stone and placed it on the empty seat high in the air. The stone pushed the seat down, so Sara soared up high. But there she stayed.

"I want to go up and down," complained Sara. *"Going up is only half the fun."*

So Steve took the stone off the low seat, and Sara's seat came smashing to the ground. WHAPP!! *"I give up,"* said Sara, rubbing her sore tail. *"There must be a special secret way to ride a seesaw up and down."*

"I guess so," said Steve. *"It's just too bad that the two of us will probably never be able to figure it out..."*

Comprehension Questions

• Who was Sara Snake watching in the beginning of the story?
• What did Sara play with on the playground? Why did she think the seesaw would be the most fun?
• Why couldn't Sara ride up and down on the seesaw? Who tried to help her? How did Steve try to help?
• Do you think Sara and Steve will figure out how to use the seesaw? What would you tell them to do?

Follow-up Activities

Squiggle Art

Draw a series of large S-shapes on a piece of paper. Duplicate one paper for each child, and tell the group to decorate their S-shapes to resemble objects, animals, or people.

See some Seesaws

Observe a seesaw in action. Note which children are able to balance and operate it smoothly. Back inside, look for other games, toys, and materials which rely on balance--a scale, a rocking chair, a picture hanging on a nail. Help children create their own seesaw effects with building blocks.

"Snake" Up on 'Em

Have one child sit in chair with back to the group. Have remaining children slither up to chair trying to touch child before he turns around. The "snake" who reaches a child without being detected becomes the next "child in the chair."

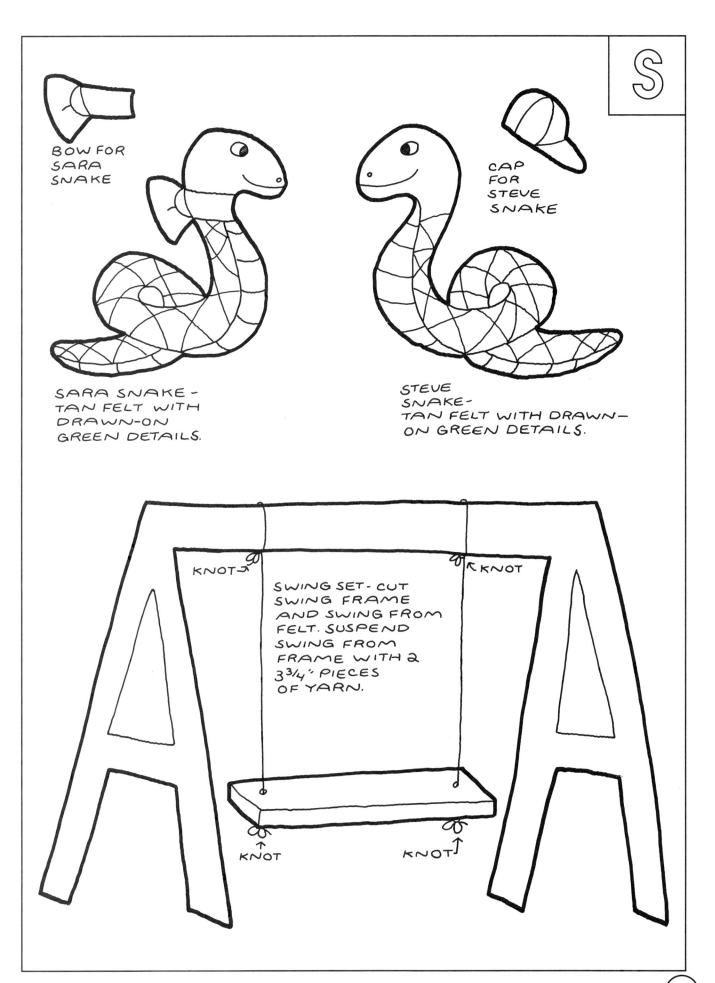

BOW FOR
SARA
SNAKE

CAP
FOR
STEVE
SNAKE

SARA SNAKE -
TAN FELT WITH
DRAWN-ON
GREEN DETAILS.

STEVE
SNAKE -
TAN FELT WITH DRAWN-
ON GREEN DETAILS.

KNOT

KNOT

SWING SET - CUT
SWING FRAME
AND SWING FROM
FELT. SUSPEND
SWING FROM
FRAME WITH 2
3¾" PIECES
OF YARN.

KNOT

KNOT

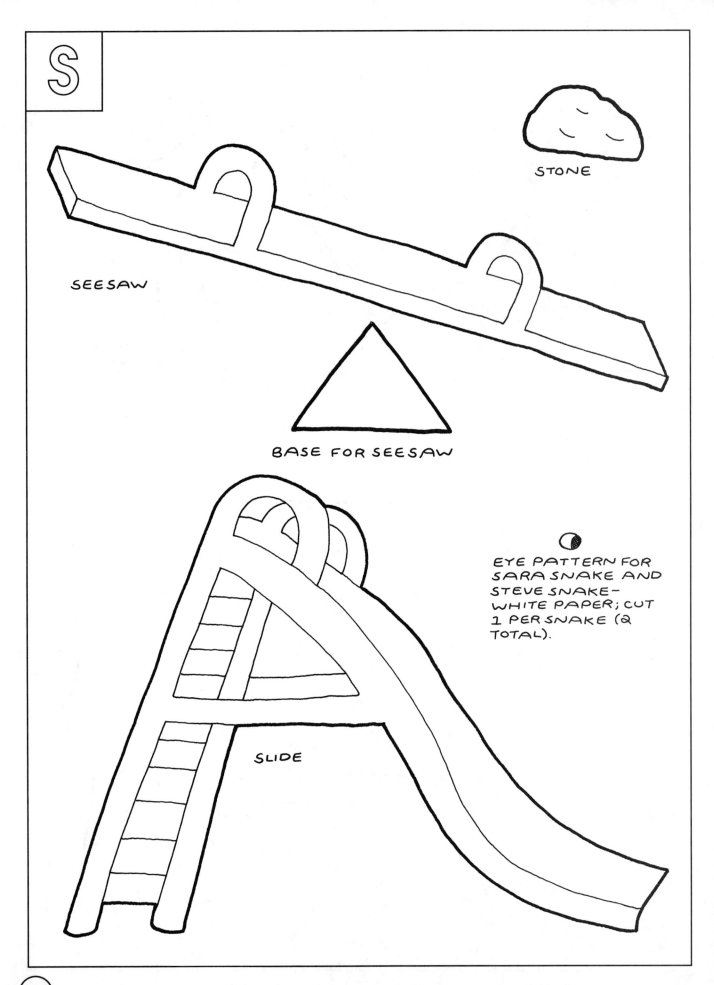

STONE

SEESAW

BASE FOR SEESAW

EYE PATTERN FOR
SARA SNAKE AND
STEVE SNAKE—
WHITE PAPER; CUT
1 PER SNAKE (2
TOTAL).

SLIDE

Timothy Turtle, Tattletale

Timothy Turtle was a tattletale. He never missed a chance to tell the teacher when one of his friends had done something wrong. He was always on the lookout for ways to get others in trouble.

When Tammy Turkey spilled the box of triangles, Timothy tattled. When Tina Terrier stuck her tongue out at the teacher, Timothy tattled, and when Teddy Bear tore his trousers, Timothy tattled.

One school day, when Timothy was home sick with a temperature, the teacher, Mr. Tiger asked the class to talk about the problem of Timothy's tattling.

"I hate when Timothy tattles," said Tammy Turkey. *"Doesn't he want me to be his friend?"*

"I get angry when Timothy tattles," added Tina Terrier. *"Doesn't Timothy ever make mistakes himself?"*

"Sometimes, Timothy can be nice," said Teddy Bear, *"but not when he tattles!"*

Mr. Tiger listened to the class, and then he told them something they never thought of.

"Timothy wants everyone to like him, but he's afraid that he's not good enough. Instead of trying to look for friends, he looks for everybody else's mistakes. I think that if Timothy felt better about himself, he would be a better friend to all of you!"

"Why don't we have a surprise party for Timothy?" suggested Teddy Bear. *"We can serve treats of toast and tuna and tangerine tea. We can make him feel happy again and we can show him that we want to be his friends."*

Everyone agreed that the surprise party idea was terrific. The next day, the class gathered behind the tall tree to make their plans. Seeing everyone else behind the tree, Timothy Turtle thought that the kids were telling mean secrets.

"Boys and girls," said Mr. Tiger, *"what were you doing to hurt Timothy's feelings?"*

"We were planning Timothy's surprise party," they said together.

"What surprise party?" said Timothy, not believing his little turtle ears.

"We want to be your friends," they said. *"We want you to stop tattling on us!"*

"I guess by tattling I spoiled the surprise, didn't I?" he said. *"But that will be the last time I tattle! I've learned my lesson for good!"*

TANGERINE
TEA –
ORANGE
FELT

TOAST-
TAN
FELT

TUNA
(IN CAN)-
GREY FELT

Comprehension Questions

• What was Timothy Turtle's problem? What is a tattletale?
• How did the other animals in the story feel about Timothy.
What did the teacher tell them about Timothy?
• What did the animals do to help make Timothy feel better?
Did the plan work?
• Do you think Timothy will ever tattle again?

Follow-up Activities

Play Tattletale

One child sits in a chair with his back to the group, his eyes closed. Another child says, *"Timothy Turtle is a tattletale."* The child in the chair has three chances to guess who is being a tattletale.

Have Tuna on Toast

With the group, mix tuna fish with mayonnaise, chopped celery, and carrots. Toast bread (one slice for four servings), and spread bread with tuna mixture. Cut bread into fourths and serve.

Recognize a Tattle When You Hear One

Tell the children that they are going to listen for examples of true tattletales. Tell them that you are going to say some sentences and instruct them to raise their hands when they hear a tattletale. Some sample sentences are:

"Teacher, Johnny said a bad word." (a tattle)
"Teacher, I want a drink of water, please."
"Teacher, Sally ate two cookies." (a tattle)
"Teacher, May I play with the paints?"
"Teacher, Tommy ran in the halls." (a tattle)

You may want to differentiate between the concept of telling on someone for the sake of getting them in trouble and asking for adult help in working out a situation. Even after an explanation pointing out the differences between the situations, children will often be unable to differentiate themselves, and so they will require ongoing reminders.

BOX FOR TRIANGLES-
CUT ALONG BROKEN
LINES SO TRIANGLES
CAN FIT INSIDE,

TRIANGLES

EYE PATTERN FOR TIMOTHY TURTLE, MR. TIGER, AND TAMMY TURKEY— WHITE PAPER; CUT 1 PER ANIMAL (3 TOTAL).

COLLAR AND TIE FOR MR. TIGER— WHITE FELT

TURTLE SHELL FOR TIMOTHY— OLIVE GREEN FELT

TIMOTHY TURTLE— GREEN FELT

MR. TIGER— TAN FELT; USE BROWN MARKER TO DRAW IN DETAILS.

T

TAMMY TURKEY-RED FELT;
USE BROWN MARKER TO
DRAW IN DETAILS.

TEDDY BEAR-TAN FELT

BEAK FOR
TAMMY
TURKEY-
YELLOW
FELT

TORN TROUSERS FOR
TEDDY BEAR

"CLAWS" FOR
TAMMY TURKEY-
YELLOW FELT

TALL TREE-GREEN FELT

BOW FOR
TINA
TERRIER

TONGUE FOR
TINA TERRIER-
PINK FELT

TINA TERRIER-
WHITE FELT; USE
BLACK MARKER TO
DRAW IN DETAILS.

TREE TRUNK-BROWN
FELT; GLUE TO BOTTOM
OF TALL TREE.

The Unusual Umbrella

Once upon a time, there was an unusual umbrella that didn't like to get wet! Whenever he heard the pitter-patter of rain-drops, he would hide any where he thought his owner, Uncle Upper, would not see him. Sometimes, he hid *under* the rain-boots, sometimes he hid high *up* on a shelf.

Because the unusual umbrella was always undercover and very difficult to find, Uncle decided to buy a new umbrella to hang in the closet. The new umbrella was unbelievably beautiful. She had polka dots upon her fabric and stripes underneath.

When the next rain storm came, the unusual umbrella hid high upon the shelf and peeked over to watch what would happen. He heard the closet door being unlocked. Then, he saw Uncle unhook the new umbrella from her closet hook and unsnap her strap and pop her up and open.

The new umbrella looked very brave as she headed out into the dark storm that day. The unusual umbrella couldn't wait for the new umbrella to return so that he could find out what the world looked like. Finally, he saw Uncle hang the new umbrella back upon her hook.

"How was the rain storm?" asked the unusual umbrella.

"It was unusually lovely," whispered the new umbrella "Soft raindrops were everywhere! They fell upon grass and houses. They ran in tiny rivers under flowers and trees and they made puddles for children to splash in."

"Didn't you mind getting wet?" asked the unusual umbrella.

"Oh, no!" answered the new umbrella. "The rain felt cool and fresh upon my cover. And I like being a helper, keeping Uncle nice and dry under me."

The unusual umbrella thought about all the nice things that the new umbrella had told him about the rain. He also thought about how lonely he had felt when the new umbrella had gone out into the storm without him.

The next time he heard raindrops, the unusual umbrella did not hide under the rainboots or up high upon the shelf. Instead, the unusual umbrella tried to be unusually brave, and he hung straight and tall right next to the new umbrella waiting to go out under the rain. When the closet door was unlocked, the two umbrellas saw *two* people standing there. Uncle had a friend over for a visit and each man needed an umbrella for a walk in the rain.

And so the two friends and the two umbrellas walked together down the rainy path. The unusual umbrella was never lonely or frightened again.

Comprehension Questions

• What did the unusual umbrella do when it rained? Why?
• Why do you think the unusual umbrella was afraid of the rain?
• How does the unusual umbrella feel about the new umbrella? How can you tell?
• In the end of the story, the unusual umbrella goes out into the rain with the new umbrella. Do you think he is still afraid? How do you know?

Follow-up Activities

Umbrella Movement

Try this movement exercise on a rainy day when outdoor play is an impossibility. Tell the children to pretend that they are umbrellas tightly closed up in a dark closet. (One arm extended up can represent the curved handle of the umbrella.) It begins to rain outside, slowly at first, then faster. (Beat raindrop rhythms on a drum.) Someone takes each umbrella from the closet and pops it open. (Children extend arms to represent open umbrellas.) Once open, the umbrellas are carried high (tiptoes), low (bend knees), fast, slow, to the left, or to the right. Finally, the umbrellas come home again, are set on the floor to dry, and are then closed up tightly and hung back in the quiet, dark closet.

Drippy Paintings

Have children paint familiar outdoor scenes and then sprinkle them with raindrops created by dipping a toothbrush in blue paint, holding the brush over the paintings, and raking the bristles with a wooden craft stick. Be sure to wear "smock raincoats" for this splashy activity.

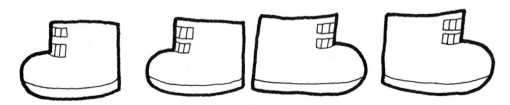

RAIN BOOTS - FOR CLOSET

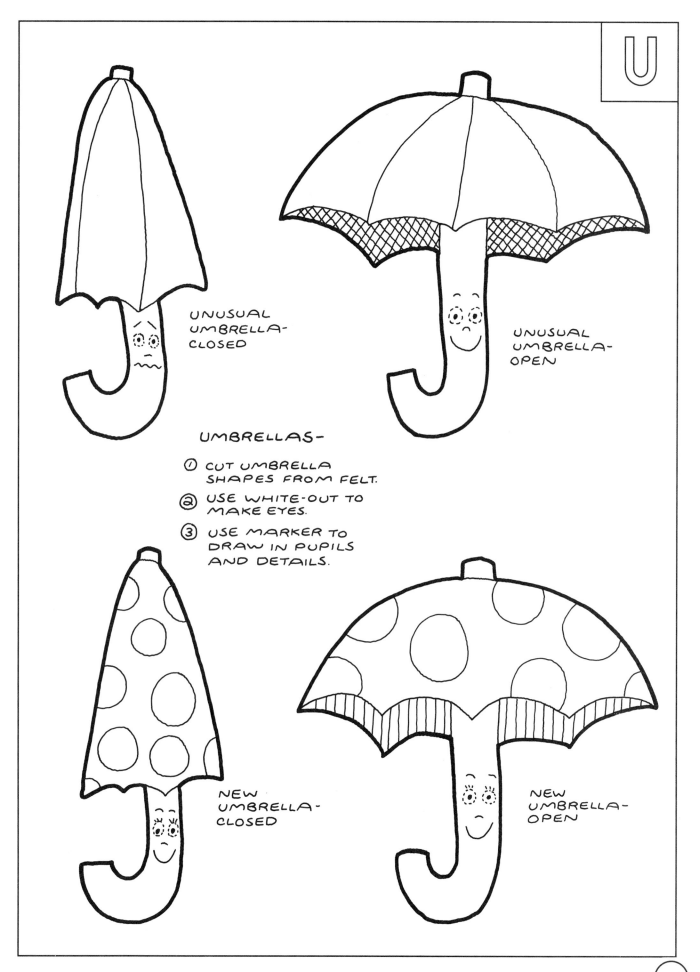

UNUSUAL
UMBRELLA-
CLOSED

UNUSUAL
UMBRELLA-
OPEN

UMBRELLAS-

① CUT UMBRELLA
SHAPES FROM FELT.

② USE WHITE-OUT TO
MAKE EYES.

③ USE MARKER TO
DRAW IN PUPILS
AND DETAILS.

NEW
UMBRELLA-
CLOSED

NEW
UMBRELLA-
OPEN

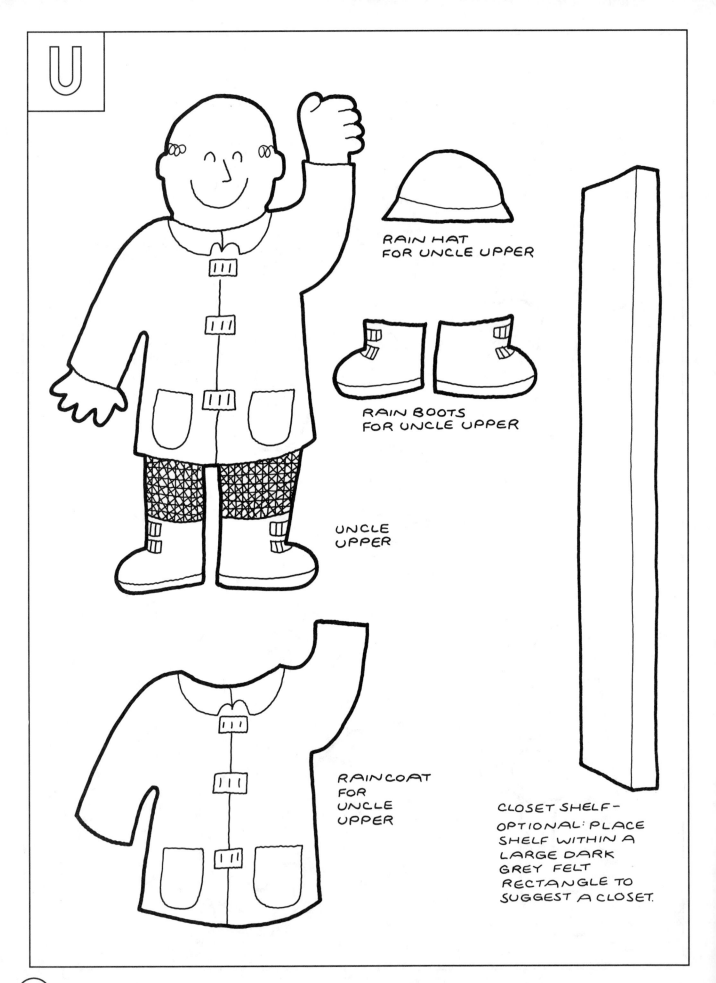

U

RAIN HAT
FOR UNCLE UPPER

RAIN BOOTS
FOR UNCLE UPPER

UNCLE
UPPER

RAINCOAT
FOR
UNCLE
UPPER

CLOSET SHELF -
OPTIONAL: PLACE
SHELF WITHIN A
LARGE DARK
GREY FELT
RECTANGLE TO
SUGGEST A CLOSET.

The Valuable Valentine

Once upon a time, there were two children named Victor and Vivian who were best friends.

Victor and Vivian enjoyed giving each other cards and gifts, so, when Valentine's Day came, they were excited to make paper valentines for each other, and they each planned their valentines in secret.

Victor wanted his valentine for Vivian to be special. He carefully cut out a beautiful card and, with his violet crayon, drew onto it a vase of violets. He decorated the edges with violet lace, and tried to think of something to print to her inside. All he could think of was this poem:

> *Roses are red*
> *Violets are blue*
> *I ran out of tape*
> *So, I had to use glue!*

The ugly poem didn't sound like it belonged inside of a valentine, but at least the card *looked* pretty.

Vivian also wanted her valentine for Victor to be special. She carefully cut out a card, but it looked very wiggly. Then, she tried to decorate it with her violet crayon, but it just looked like scribble-scrabble. When she was done, she thought of a poem to print inside:

> *Roses are red*
> *Violets are blue*
> *There is no friend more special*
> *Than Y-O-U !!*

The ugly card didn't look like it belonged on the outside of the poem, but at least the card *sounded* pretty!

On Valentine's Day, the two friends held their surprise valentines behind their backs. *"Happy Valentine's Day!"* they said together and out came their cards.

"Your poem is prettier than my poem," said Victor.

"And, your card is prettier than my card," said Vivian.

"Let's put the best part of our cards together!" they said at once.

And so, to make the nicest valentine ever, they used the *outside* of Victor's card and the *inside* of Vivian's card. Of course, now that there's only one card, they have to share it between them, but neither Victor nor Vivian has ever minded sharing even one little bit.

Comprehension Questions

- Who are the two children in the story? What holiday are they going to celebrate? What surprise are they planning for each other?
- What is a valentine?
- What is Victor able to do well when he tries to make a valentine? What is Vivian able to do well when she tries to make a valentine?
- Do you think that Victor and Vivian are good friends? How do you know?

Follow-up Activities

Send Valentines

Even if it's not officially the season, it's always nice to send and receive a valentine. Friends or relatives, who don't expect to receive valentines in June or October, will welcome the surprise and will cherish the loving messages inside.

Decorate Vests

Use brown grocery bags to create paper vests. Cut down the center of the front panel of each bag, and cut a circle in the bottom of the bag for the head. Position a bag on each child, and mark sides of bag for armhole cuts. Cut armholes for child, and give bag to child to decorate with paints, crayons or markers. These vests can resemble Indian leather vests, or may be used for costumes for an informal class play.

Make Vanilla Shakes

Place milk (two cups), honey (to taste), nutmeg (a dash), and vanilla (a splash) into blender. Add three or four ice cubes. Blend on high setting and serve with vanilla wafers.

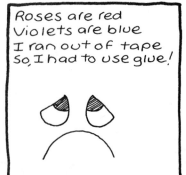

POETRY PAGES-

① CUT 2" X 2" PIECE OF PAPER (FOR 1 CARD).

② WRITE POEM ON PAPER AND DRAW ON FACE.

③ GLUE SMALL PIECE OF FELT ON BACK OF PAPER SO IT CAN BE ATTACHED AND THEN BE REMOVED FROM INSIDE OF CARD.

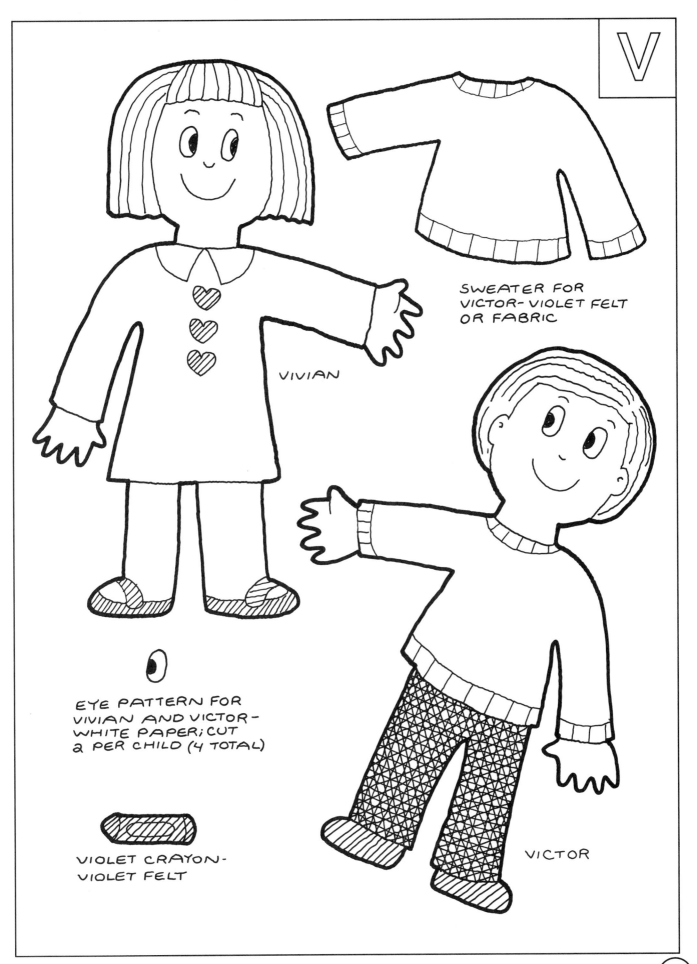

SWEATER FOR
VICTOR- VIOLET FELT
OR FABRIC

VIVIAN

EYE PATTERN FOR
VIVIAN AND VICTOR-
WHITE PAPER; CUT
2 PER CHILD (4 TOTAL)

VIOLET CRAYON-
VIOLET FELT

VICTOR

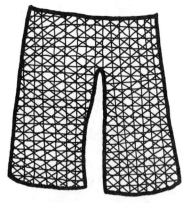

PANTS FOR VICTOR-
FELT OR FABRIC

DRESS FOR VIVIAN-
VIOLET FELT OR FABRIC

V

PRETTY
VALENTINE
(FRONT OF
CARD)

UGLY
VALENTINE
(FRONT OF
CARD)

VALENTINES

① CUT A 4" × 2" PIECE OF PAPER IN HALF.

② GLUE 1 SMALL PIECE OF FELT TO BACK OF CARD
AND 1 SMALL PIECE OF FELT INSIDE CARD.

←FELT   ←FELT

③ FOR PRETTY VALENTINE-USE A VIOLET CRAYON TO
DRAW A VASE AND VIOLETS AND TO COLOR IN A PAPER
DOILY ONTO FRONT OF CARD TO RESEMBLE A VIOLET LACE
FRAME.

④ FOR UGLY VALENTINE-CUT WIGGLY OUTLINE AROUND
CARD.USE A VIOLET CRAYON TO MAKE A SCRIBBLE
SCRABBLE DESIGN ON FRONT.

The Witch Race

Once upon a time, there was a wicked witch named Witchy who lived in a huge haunted house. In the house next door, there lived a witch named Wilma. Wilma was not like Witchy who tried to frighten children. Instead, Wilma was a warm and wonderful witch who only liked to wish people well.

Witchy thought that Wilma was weird. She tried to make fun of her and hurt her feelings. She called her *"Wimpy Wilma."* Every time Witchy saw Wilma weeding her garden, she pointed her crooked, green fingers at her and laughed.

Wilma was not wimpy, but she was very wise. She soon thought of a clever way to turn Witchy into warm and wonderful witch like herself.

One Wednesday, as she was weeding her garden, she heard the familiar mean laughter. She turned around and, sure enough, there was Witchy pointing her crooked fingers and making fun of her.

Wilma said, *"I'm tired of being different from you. I would like to race you on my magic broomstick. If I lose, I promise I will become as wicked as you are; but if I win; you must promise to grant me just one magical wish."*

Witchy was wild with delight. She thought that Wilma was not wicked enough to ride her broomstick very quickly. She thought that she would win for sure, so she agreed to the broomstick race. It was to be held the following Wednesday night.

Witchy went inside to make some witch stew. She didn't practice her broom-riding. She thought she would win for sure.

But, Wilma Witch knew that she *had* to win the broomstick race. So, every night for a whole week, Wilma worked on her broomstick. At her workbench, she added secret pieces of wood and wire to make her broomstick the best in all the land.

Finally, the night of the race had come. Witchy and Wilma met at the old willow tree. At midnight, the race began.

At first, Witchy was in front of Wilma. She rode on the wind like an expert. She rode wild and fast. Just when it seemed certain that she would win, the wind died down, and Witchy was forced to slow down. But, Wilma Witch was not forced to slow down; with wire, she had built special wings onto her broomstick, and these wings now helped to keep her broom flying high and strong. With Witchy angrily following behind, Wilma rode straight for the finish line proving that she was the winner!

"I suppose you want that one wish now," growled Witchy, thinking that Wilma would want all of her gold treasures.

"My wish," said Wilma, *"is that you will no longer be wicked and wild, but instead you will be a warm and wonderful friend of mine."*

And they returned home to weed the garden--together.

WITCHES STEW

WEEDS IN GARDEN

Comprehension Questions

- How was Wilma different from Witchy witch? Why do you think she was different?
- What do you think of Wilma's idea for a broomstick race?
- Why do you think Wilma won the race? Do you think Witchy will ever race Wilma again?
- Why do you think Wilma's wish was to be friends with Witchy?

Follow-up Activities

Have a Witch Relay Race

Divide your group into two teams of witches and have them stand in two parallel lines. At the opposite end of the room or playground, place two cone-shaped witch hats. When you say "Witches Fly!" the first child in each line must run to the hat, run round the hat and then run back and touch the next child in line. The first group of "witches" to finish the race wins.

Make Witch Mobiles

To illustrate the wicked and the wonderful sides of the witches in the story, give each child two solid green paper plates (available at party shops). On the blackboard, show children how to draw some facial features. (For artistic assistance, use *Ed Emberly's Drawing Book of Faces*.) Then, let them decorate one plate with a kind face and one plate with a wicked face. Glue the plates back-to-back, punch a hole in the top, thread with black yarn, and hang.

Plant Weed Gardens

In the spring and summer, transplant weeds to containers-- clay pots, plastic tubs. A small paper witch puppet (Duplicate, cut and color witch flannelboard piece.) attached to a craft stick may be stuck in the soil to tend the garden.

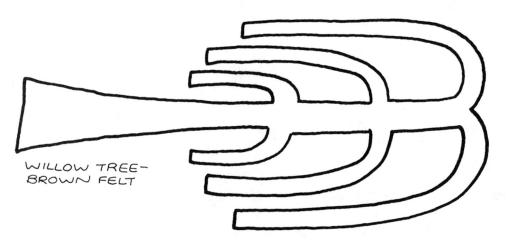

WILLOW TREE- BROWN FELT

WILLOW TREE LEAF~ GREEN FELT; CUT SEVERAL AND GLUE ONTO WILLOW BRANCHES.

BROOMSTICKS FOR WILMA AND WITCHY WITCH- TAN FELT; CUT 1 BROOMSTICK PER WITCH (Q TOTAL).

WINGS FOR WILMA WITCH'S BROOM- TAN FELT; PLACE ON EITHER SIDE OF WILMA'S BROOM.

FLOWER DECORATION FOR WILMA'S DRESS

FLOWERS FOR WILMA'S HAT

EYE PATTERN FOR WILMA WITCH- WHITE PAPER

WILMA WITCH'S FACE- GREEN FELT; GLUE ON YARN FOR HAIR.

WILMA WITCH- ASSEMBLED

WILMA'S HANDS- GREEN FELT

W

HAT FOR WILMA AND
WITCHY WITCH-DARK
GREY FELT; CUT 1 PER
WITCH (2 TOTAL)

BODY FOR WITCHY AND WILMA WITCH-
DARK GREY FELT; CUT 1 PER WITCH
(2 TOTAL)

EYE PATTERN
FOR WITCHY
WITCH-WHITE
PAPER

WITCHY WITCH'S
FACE- GREEN FELT;
GLUE ON YARN
FOR HAIR.

WITCHY
WITCH'S
HANDS-
GREEN
FELT

WITCHY WITCH-ASSEMBLED

Xavier and the Xylophone

Once upon a time, there was a little boy named Xavier who loved music. He loved to sing songs, listen to instruments, and play records. Most of all, Xavier loved to play the xylophone.

The school's music teacher, Mr. Excellent wanted all the children in school to take turns playing instruments. Xavier waited patiently for his turn to play the xylophone, and finally, the exciting day came.

Because Xavier loved the xylophone so much, he was able to play well. When it was time for him to play a different instrument, he begged Mr. Excellent to let him keep playing only the xylophone.

Mr. Excellent decided that, for just this once, he would allow Xavier to keep playing the xylophone. He told Xavier that if he practiced hard, he just might be able to play the xylophone in the school's music concert.

Xavier practiced playing every day and every night. Soon, he played well enough to play in the school's music concert.

The morning of the music concert, Xavier decided to practice one more time. He went to the music room, picked up the xylophone and---crash! He dropped the instrument on his foot.

"Ouch, ouch!" cried Xavier loudly. Mr. Excellent came running to help, saw what happened, and took Xavier to the hospital.

At the hospital, Xavier met Dr. Examine who looked at his foot. *"I need to take an X-ray, a picture of the inside of your foot,"* said Dr. Examine.

"This kind of picture will show me the bones of your foot. It will tell me if the xylophone broke one of your bones. The X-ray will help me fix your foot as good as new."

Xavier was a bit frightened, but he liked Doctor Examine. The foot X-ray didn't hurt one little bit, and soon Xavier's foot was bandaged up to help it heal. *"Your foot will be better soon,"* said Dr. Examine, *"but you will need to rest in the hospital until tomorrow."*

"But my music concert is tonight," said Xavier sadly. *"I was going to play my xylophone for the whole school."* Then, his face brightened. *"I know,"* he smiled, *"I'll just have the concert here in the hospital. Instead of playing my xylophone for the whole school, I'll play for the whole hospital."*

And everyone agreed it was the most excellent xylophone concert anyone at the hospital had *ever* experienced.

Comprehension Questions

• What did Xavier love to do in school?
• Why did Xavier practice the xylophone so much?
• What happened to Xavier the day of the music concert. What were some of Xavier's feelings when he hurt himself?
• What is an x-ray? How do x-rays help doctors know what is wrong with people?

Follow-up Activities

Examine X-rays

Arrange to visit a dentist's or doctor's office with your children to observe and discuss x-rays. Inquire about the possibility of taking some old x-rays back to school to keep and display.

Play Xylophones

Chances are, your children are familiar with toy xylophones. Arrange to borrow and let your childen experiment with a standard-sized xylophone. (Try contacting school music department or music stores.)

Turn Lemons Into Lemonade

Xavier has some bad luck, but turns the unhappy situation into a red letter day. Offer your children some typical disappointing scenarios--a rained-out picnic, a missed birthday party, a sold-out ice cream flavor--and ask them to brainstorm ways to help make the best of a bad situation.

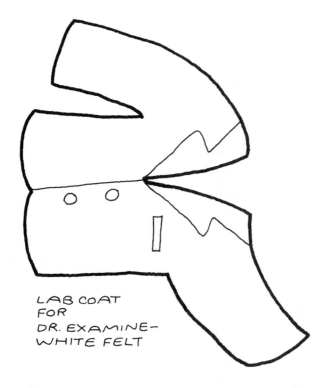

LAB COAT
FOR
DR. EXAMINE-
WHITE FELT

MALLETS FOR
XYLOPHONE- TAN FELT

XYLOPHONE - GREY FELT; COLOR IN SPACES BETWEEN BARS.

STAND FOR
XYLOPHONE—
TAN FELT; PLACE
XYLOPHONE
ON STAND.

SHOES AND
SOCKS FOR
XAVIER

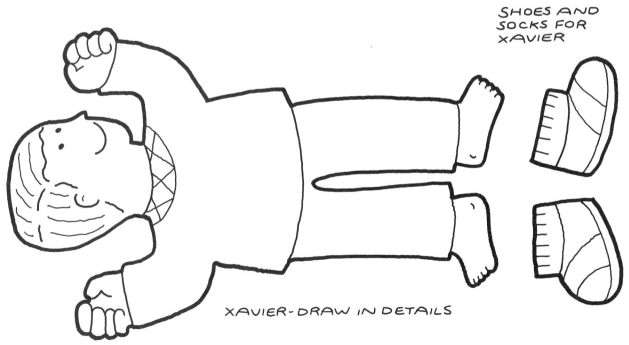

XAVIER - DRAW IN DETAILS

GLUE ON A PIECE OF FOIL

DR. EXAMINE-
DRAW IN
DETAILS.

X-RAY OF
FOOT-
WHITE PAPER
WITH A
SMALL
PIECE OF
FELT GLUED
ON BACK.

MR.
EXCELLENT-
DRAW IN
DETAILS.

Yolanda the Yeller

Once upon a time there was a girl about your age named Yolanda. Yolanda was usually a good girl, but she did have one big problem. Whenever she got angry, Yolanda would yell at the top fo her lungs. She would yell so loud that no one could understand what she had to say.

One day, Yolanda brought her yo-yo to school. It was a beautiful yellow yo-yo which hung down on a piece of yellow yarn. She couldn't wait to show her friends at recess, but when recess came, the yo-yo was gone!

"Somebody swiped my yo-yo!" yelled Yolanda. But no one listened to her yell. So, she yelled louder. *"Somebody swiped my yo-yo!"*

Still no one listened, so she yelled even louder. *"SOMEBODY SWIPED MY YO-YO AND I'M TELLING THE TEACHER!"*

Yolanda ran in to her teacher, Mr. Yesterday, and she yelled her message right in his ear, *"Somebody swiped my Yo-Yo!"*

Mr. Yesterday could not understand one word of Yolanda's yells, but he did know that her voice hurt his ears.

"I can't understand your words Yolanda, but I want to help you. Here is a yellow crayon and paper. Draw for me a picture of what is upsetting you."

So Yolanda took the yellow crayon and began to draw a picture of her beautiful, yellow yo-yo with the yellow yarn. A big tear ran down her cheek. *"I can't find my yellow yo-yo,"* she sniffled. *"I think somebody swiped it."*

Mr. Yesterday opened his desk drawer. *"I found this yo-yo in the yard of the school,"* he said kindly. *"Do you think it could be yours?"*

And, sure enough, there was Yolanda's yellow yo-yo with the yellow yarn.

"Here, Yolanda, take your yo-yo," said Mr. Yesterday. *"And the next time you feel like yelling, draw your feelings instead."*

"THANK YOU, MR. YESTERDAY!" yelled Yolanda.

And then, ever so softly, she winked.

Comprehension Questions

- What did Yolanda do when she was angry? What do you do when they are angry?
- What did Yolanda lose at school? How do you think she felt?
- Why do you think Yolanda told her teacher her problem?
- What did Mr. Yesterday try to teach Yolanda? What do you think she will do the next time she gets angry?

Follow-up Activities

Spin a Yarn

With children, cut cardboard circles six inches in diameter and mark the center. Have them spread one side evenly with white craft glue. Beginning in the exact center of the circle, have children pres, and wind yellow yarn in a concentric pattern covering the cardboard. (You may wish to cut yarn into small pieces, and you may want to provide a variety of yellow yarn types.) When a circle is completely covered, let dry and hang from a ribbon for a necklace or decoration.

Create "Yippie!" Books

Have children dictate sentences about events or happenings that make them yell, *"Yippie!"* Illustrate these and collect pages to make *"Yippie"* books.

Have a Yellow Yard Party

Weather permitting, invite everyone to dress in yellow for an outdoor bash with a yellow theme. For munching, try yellow kebobs: skew alternating bits of swiss cheese, bananas, and pineapple. Serve with crackers and lemonade.

PAPER WITH YELLOW YO-YO DRAWN ON IT – GLUE A SMALL PIECE OF FELT TO BACK.

YELLOW CRAYON-YELLOW FELT

13/4" PIECE OF YELLOW YARN- GLUE 1 END BEHIND FELT YO-YO.

YELLOW YO-YO-YELLOW FELT

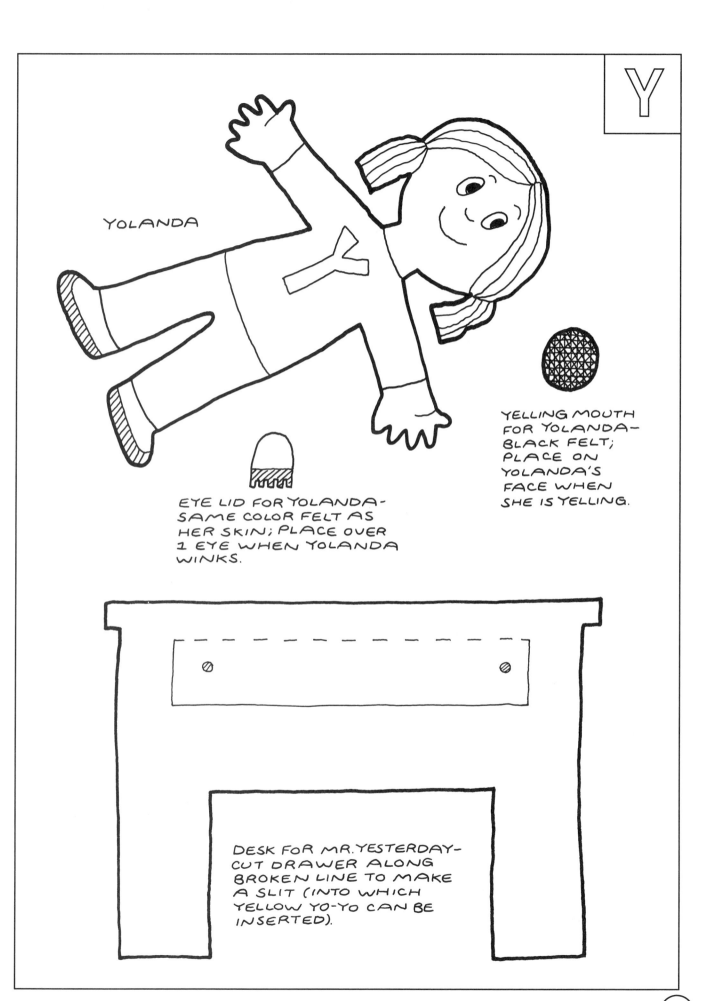

Y

YOLANDA

YELLING MOUTH FOR YOLANDA— BLACK FELT; PLACE ON YOLANDA'S FACE WHEN SHE IS YELLING.

EYE LID FOR YOLANDA— SAME COLOR FELT AS HER SKIN; PLACE OVER 1 EYE WHEN YOLANDA WINKS.

DESK FOR MR. YESTERDAY— CUT DRAWER ALONG BROKEN LINE TO MAKE A SLIT (INTO WHICH YELLOW YO-YO CAN BE INSERTED).

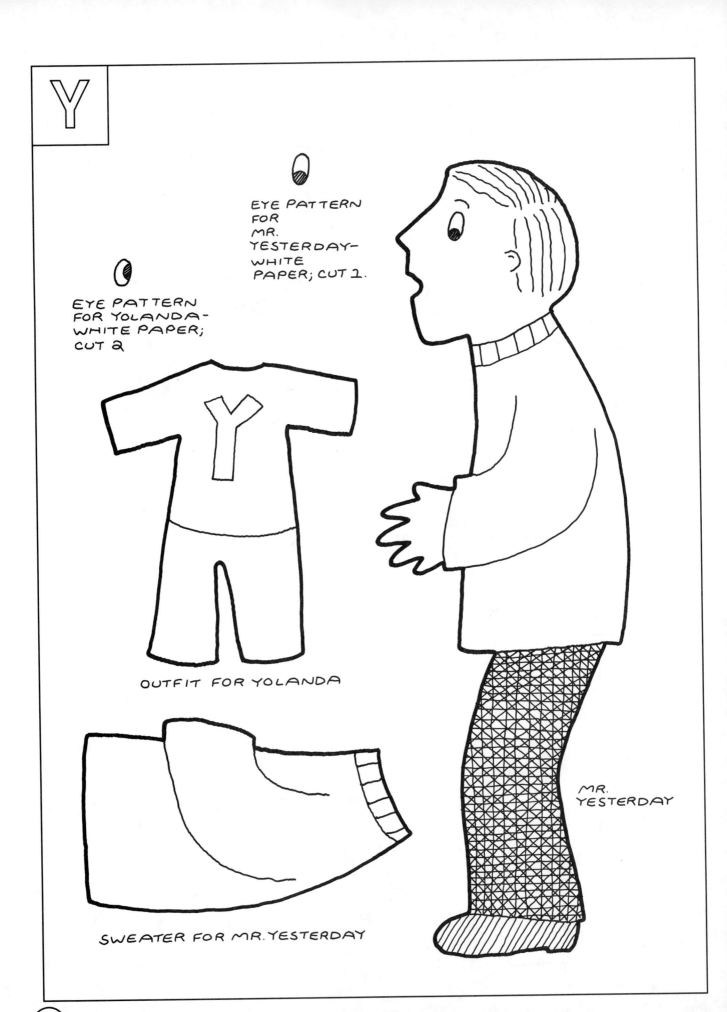

EYE PATTERN
FOR
MR.
YESTERDAY-
WHITE
PAPER; CUT 1.

EYE PATTERN
FOR YOLANDA-
WHITE PAPER;
CUT 2

OUTFIT FOR YOLANDA

SWEATER FOR MR. YESTERDAY

MR.
YESTERDAY

Zeek Zebra and the Zipper

Once upon a time, there was a baby zebra named Zeek. Zeek lived in the zoo with his mother, Mrs. Zebra.

When the children visiting the zoo pointed and waved, Mrs. Zebra and Zeek would both stand tall and wave back with their long tails.

Of all the children who visited the zoo, Zeek Zebra loved Zach the best. Zach was a little boy who came to the zoo everyday. Even on days when it was cold and windy, Zach, bundled in his winter coat with the pile-lined hood, could be found watching the zebra family.

One day in spring, the sun shone warmer than usual. While Zach stood visiting the zebras, he zipped off his warm winter coat with the warm winter hood and hung it over his arm.

Zeek couldn't believe his zebra eyes. He had never seen a boy take off his coat before. He didn't know that coats could be unzipped.

Suddenly, Zeek decided that he too wanted to unzip his coat.

Zeek began to look for his coat's zipper. He looked on his back. He looked under his legs. He looked on top of his nose, and he *even* looked behind his ears. But try as he might, Zeek could not find even *one* zipper!

"Mommy," said Zeek, "I want to be like Zach. I want to zip off my coat and I can't find my zipper!"

"My dear little Zeek," said Mother, "zebra's don't have zippers on their coats. You have a beautiful zigzag coat and you should wear it proudly all year long."

"But I hate my zigzag stripes," said Zeek. "And I hate my coat, too!"

Later that day, when Zeek saw Zach waving to him, the baby zebra tried to stand tall, but it was not easy to do. Just then, the zoo keeper came over to talk to Zach. "Tell me Zach, why do you like the zebra so much?" said the zoo keeper. "Is it because they remind you of horses, or is it because you like to see them wave their tails?"

"They do remind me of horses and I do like to watch them wave their tails. But if you ask me," said Zach, "the best thing about zebras are their zigzags. I'm sure glad they never unzip their coats like we do!"

With those words, Zach saw that Zeek seemed to stand taller and prouder than ever before. He even thought he saw the baby zebra smile.

And he was right.

Comprehension Questions

• Who was Zeek? Where did Zeek live?
• Who was Zach? What did he wear when he visited the zoo? What kind of boy do you think Zach was?
• Why do you think Zeek Zebra wanted to be like Zach? How did Zeek feel when he found out that he could not unzip his zigzag stripes?
• How did Zeek's feelings change at the end of the story?

Follow-up Activities

Zig Zag Around

Walk in a silly zigzag pattern on the playground or around the room. Choose different children to be the "Zigzag Zebra Leader," and follow the crazy path they make to any routine destination.

Paint Zigzags

Place the zebra flannelboard pattern piece on an overhead projector. Enlarge the image to desired size and project onto paper, trace image, then paint on stripes, adding yarn for mane and tail.

Unzip Their Lip

Have children name places and things that have zippers. See how long your "Zipper List" can get. Remember to include zippers on camping equipment, camera bags, doll clothes, and furniture.

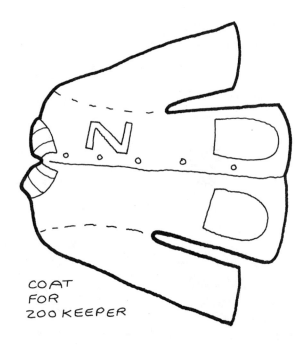

COAT
FOR
ZOO KEEPER

SMILE FOR
ZEEK ZEBRA-
SAME COLOR
AS MUZZLE;
PLACE OVER
ZEEK'S MUZZLE
WHEN HE SMILES.

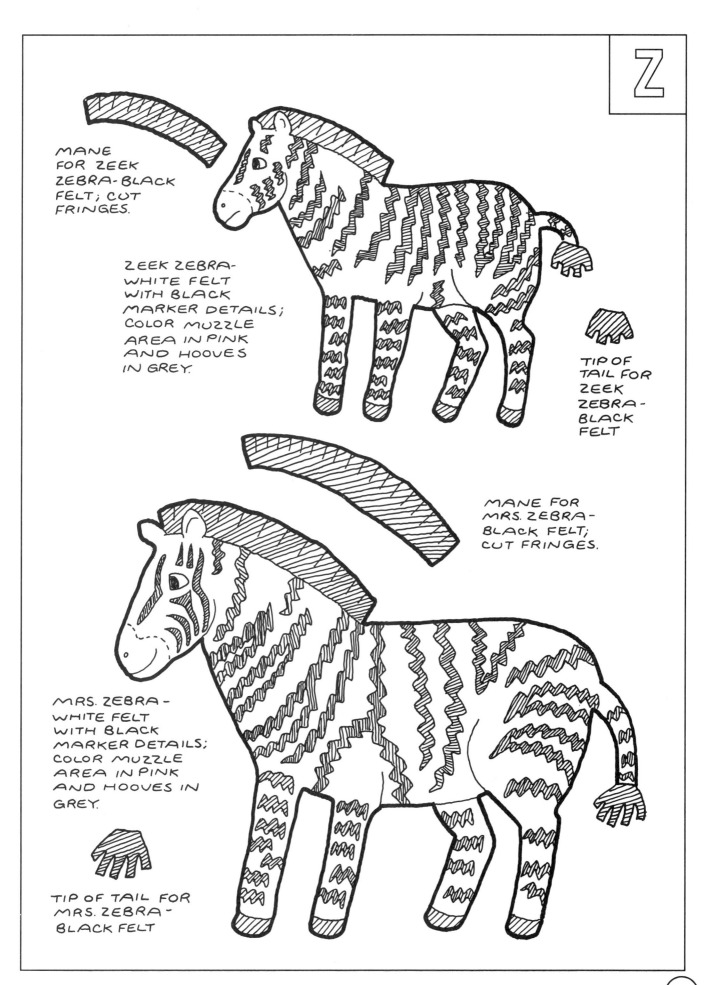

MANE FOR ZEEK ZEBRA-BLACK FELT; CUT FRINGES.

ZEEK ZEBRA-WHITE FELT WITH BLACK MARKER DETAILS; COLOR MUZZLE AREA IN PINK AND HOOVES IN GREY.

TIP OF TAIL FOR ZEEK ZEBRA-BLACK FELT

MANE FOR MRS. ZEBRA-BLACK FELT; CUT FRINGES.

MRS. ZEBRA-WHITE FELT WITH BLACK MARKER DETAILS; COLOR MUZZLE AREA IN PINK AND HOOVES IN GREY.

TIP OF TAIL FOR MRS. ZEBRA-BLACK FELT

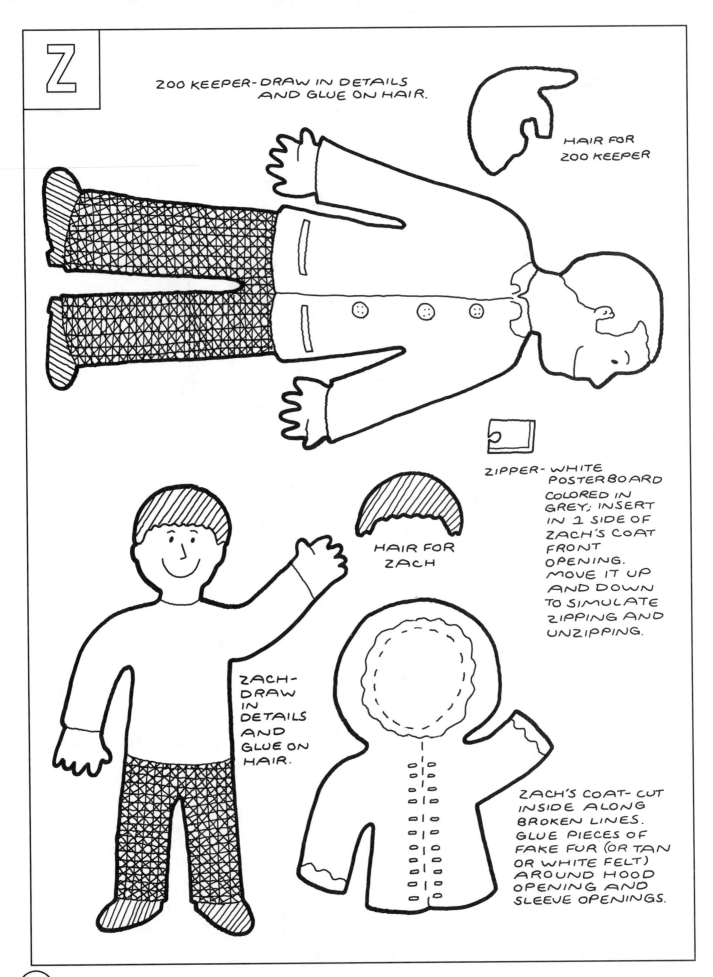

Z

ZOO KEEPER-DRAW IN DETAILS AND GLUE ON HAIR.

HAIR FOR ZOO KEEPER

ZIPPER- WHITE POSTERBOARD COLORED IN GREY; INSERT IN 1 SIDE OF ZACH'S COAT FRONT OPENING. MOVE IT UP AND DOWN TO SIMULATE ZIPPING AND UNZIPPING.

HAIR FOR ZACH

ZACH- DRAW IN DETAILS AND GLUE ON HAIR.

ZACH'S COAT- CUT INSIDE ALONG BROKEN LINES. GLUE PIECES OF FAKE FUR (OR TAN OR WHITE FELT) AROUND HOOD OPENING AND SLEEVE OPENINGS.

Q: WHERE CAN YOU FIND HUNDREDS OF CLASSROOM TESTED IDEAS *EACH MONTH* TO HELP YOUR CHILDREN LEARN AND GROW?

A: IN FIRST TEACHER

Each 16 page issue of FIRST TEACHER provides you with innovative projects to make each day an exciting new adventure. We give you ideas for toymaking, games and recipes to do with young children. We take you to the world of make believe with ideas for drama and creative movement. And experts recommend the very best books for young children in FIRST TEACHER.

FIRST TEACHER has a newspaper format, but it's something to read and save. Each issue has a topical theme, so each one adds a permanent resource of projects and ideas to your school or center.

FIRST TEACHER is written by experienced caregivers, daycare directors, and nursery teachers, so it's full of tested ideas to help you guide and motivate young children

FIRST TEACHER has been read and used by over 30,000 Early Childhood teachers. Here's what one of them, Racelle Mednikow, preschool teacher for 16 years, says:

"What a pleasure to be provided with well written, resourceful and usable ideas that can be interjected into our everyday curriculum and be of true value to each of our teachers!"

"Thank you so much for this delightful, informative newspaper."

Subscribe today! Don't miss another month of ideas, projects, and activities.

SUBSCRIBE
TODAY
AT
THIS SPECIAL
INTRODUCTORY
PRICE! **$17.95**
($6.05 OFF THE REGULAR PRICE)

Write to: FIRST TEACHER
Box 29
60 Main Street
Bridgeport, CT 06602

Or call: 1-800-341-1522
(8AM - 9PM Mon. - Fri.
9AM - 5PM Sat.)

CRAYONS CRAFTS AND CONCEPTS

by

Kathy Faggella

Art activities can teach basic concepts and be integrated into the whole curriculum. Presented in one page, easy-to-read formats, that even your children can follow, these 50+ projects will fit into each theme and subject area, you introduce. There are also suggestions for setting up an art area, making smocks, safety rules, and follow ups for each activity. Projects are designed to be reproduced and sent home for follow up, too.

TABLE OF CONTENTS

From the authors of
CRAYONS
CRAFTS
AND
CONCEPTS

CONCEPT COOKERY

by

Kathy Faggella

Through cooking experiences in the preschool classroom, children can develop basic skills and concepts. Organized by themes and concept areas, these 50+child and classroom tested recipes will fit naturally into your curriculum.

Easy-to-read, sequential recipe charts will appeal to your children as much as they do to you. Single page formats can easily be copied and sent home for parent follow up.

TABLE OF CONTENTS

TO ORDER:

Send $9.95 (plus $1 for each book's postage and handling) to:

First Teacher, Inc.
Box 29
60 Main St.
Bridgeport, CT. 06602

OR CALL: 1-800-341-1522